Autis~

Smashing It

UNLOCKING INCLUSION,
INNOVATION &
NEURODIVERGENT POTENTIAL
IN THE WORKPLACE

By

Joulie Gindi & Adrian Pascu

Visit the Official Website at: www.b-insight.co.uk

Printed in the United Kingdom

First Printing: October 2023

B-Insight Publishing

ISBN-13:

This book may be purchased for educational, business or sales promotional use. Special discounts are available on quantity purchases. For more information, please contact the publisher via email.

Email: contact@b-insight.co.uk

DISCLAIMER

While the authors and publisher have strived to be as accurate and complete as possible in the creation of this book, readers are cautioned to rely on their own judgment about their individual circumstances to act accordingly.

The authors and publisher are providing this information on an educational basis and will not be liable for damages arising out of, or in connection with, the use of the content in this book. This is a comprehensive limitation of liability that applies to all damages of any kind, including (without limitation) compensatory; direct, indirect or direct, indirect or consequential damages; loss of data, income or profit; loss of or damage to property and claims of third parties.

While all attempts have been made to verify information provided in this publication, the authors and publisher assumes no responsibility for errors, omissions, or contrary interpretation of the subject matter herein. Any perceived slights of specific persons, peoples, or organisations are unintentional. This book details the authors' own personal experiences and opinions.

You understand that this book is not intended as a substitute for consultation with a licensed professional. In the event you use any of the information in this book for yourself, which is your legal right, the authors and publisher assume no responsibility for your actions or outcomes.

TABLE OF CONTENTS

Acknowledgements ix

Introduction:
Not Fitting In, Growing Up Unaware and Diagnosis.............1

Chapter 1:
The Medical versus the Social Disability Model 13

Chapter 2:
Some Overdue Definitions 21
  Politics 24

Chapter 3:
So, What Is Autism and What Does it Feel Like? 31
  An Intro to Autism 31
  Some Strengths and Challenges: Common Traits
  Associated with Autism 49

Chapter 4:
Busting Some Common Myths and Misunderstandings ...57
  Meltdowns 58

Overthinking and Oversharing... *60*

Conversational Norms *61*

Tone of Voice... *64*

The Intimacy of Eye Contact.. *66*

Annoyingly Over-Questioning... *68*

Fault Finding and Jumping Between Subjects *70*

Detail Flooding.. *71*

Brief Answers... *72*

Silence or Mutism... *74*

No Understanding of Hierarchy... *77*

Moral Superiority Issues *78*

*The Autistic Person Refuses to Recognise that Autism
is a Disability*.. *79*

Disclosing is Not Always the Best Option *81*

Rejection Sensitivity Dysphoria (RSD).................................. *82*

Different Cultures, Different Interpretations.......................... *83*

To Finish Off… *84*

Chapter 5:
Why Does It Matter?... 89

Again, Why Does it Matter? *92*

Chapter 6:
What Do Organisations Do Wrong?...................................... 97

The Cost of Being Neurotypically Rigid.............................. *107*

Chapter 7:
Professionals on the Spectrum.. 115

Chapter 8:
The Neuro-Inclusive Workplace 123
Change the Narrative and Context *132*

Chapter 9:
Employee Journey Solutions Dive...................................135
Post-Hire... *137*
The Hiring Process.. *150*
Reflections *156*

Chapter 10:
Conclusion 159

Bonus Chapter:
Unconscious Bias and Busting It 163
The B Word *165*
Some Examples of Subtle Dynamics May Include............... *167*

Bonus, Bonus Chapter:
Tips for Parents with Kids on the Spectrum 173
Conclusion *179*

References 181

ACKNOWLEDGEMENTS

First and foremost, I would like to express my deepest gratitude to my wonderfully unique, patient and inspiring family. You loved, inspired and accepted me, even when the world of autism was still foreign to us and I didn't quite fit in or unmasked in creative ways when I was with you. You taught me to stand up for what is right, to be humane and to help others, to see the best in people, to be humble no matter what but never forget who we are, to rise when we fall, to avoid being judgemental about others, and to always be compassionate, inclusive and support those around us. I cherish your unwavering love, inspiration, care and support – even in moments of discomfort – and you doing your best with what you didn't know – you did an amazing job and continue to! My gratitude also extends to the amazing man I wrote this book with, who loved me regardless of how I initially made things difficult for him; I admire you and the work you do for those who are gifted but misunderstood or who do not fit into the rigid moulds of educational institutes or society at large.

I would also like to offer my heartfelt appreciation to those who walked alongside me in the workplace – the extraordinary managers, allies and friends who saw my potential and generously provided me with inspiration, structure and support; thank you for believing in me, nurturing me and growing me, both personally and professionally. Your guidance and encouragement have shaped me into the leader I am today.

Now, let's not forget to thank those subpar managers who sometimes make work experiences needlessly challenging and rough. While your actions were despicable and detrimental, and even included some cringeworthy moments of abuse, I choose to find a silver lining in your behaviour, and for that, I am actually grateful, so thank you; thank you for the invaluable lessons you taught me about the kind of leader I never want to become. Your negative actions showed me the true importance of being a compassionate, conscientious, trusting, and respectful leader and fuelled my determination to create a workplace that is inclusive, respectful and nurturing for all.

I also want to take a moment to acknowledge all those who have faced the adversity of harassment and discrimination; please know that I stand with you and my heart goes out to you. It is unfortunate that we have had to endure such experiences, but through it all, we have grown resilient and learnt the importance of advocating for ourselves and others. Let us stand together, united in our commitment to creating a world where everyone, regardless of their diversity, is valued and respected.

Lastly, I would like to express my gratitude to the autism community, including all the researchers, psychologists, advocates and allies. I would also like to thank all those who have shared their stories and experiences, which have encouraged me on my darkest days. Your courage in raising awareness and fostering understanding has been an ongoing source of inspiration for me. Through our collective efforts, we are breaking barriers, raising awareness and shaping a more inclusive and accepting society.

THANK YOU, one and all, for playing such an integral role in my journey. Together, we are creating a future where individuals with autism and neurodiversities can thrive, both in the workplace and beyond with social and professional justice.

With heartfelt appreciation and a dash of mischief,

Jolie

INTRODUCTION

Not Fitting In, Growing Up Unaware and Diagnosis

> *"After I spent my whole life not fitting in and not knowing what's normal or not, it felt like such a relief to get my diagnosis and finally understand what different things may mean to me compared to how they stimulate others. The next challenge was navigating how everyone around me was so used to my amazing masking skills that they did not believe my diagnosis, even after a full-on autistic burnout."*

These are the great words spoken by many late-diagnosed people on the autism spectrum...myself included!

The latest statistics suggest that at least 1 in 50 people are autistic, though the actual number may, in fact, be much higher; a few years ago, that number was 1 in 100. Certainly, the number of diagnosed autistic people has increased exponentially over recent decades, with the Centre for Disease Control and Prevention (CDC) reporting in 2020 that 1 in 36 children is autistic. There has even been talk that 1 in 25 people or more may be on the spectrum, with 9 out of 10 autistic seniors (those over 50) in the UK living undiagnosed (according to the latest research by The Lancet Regional Health Europe)[1]. Nevertheless, most aspects of the diagnosis process are still gender biased to be focused on male traits, so many women and girls go undiagnosed. Moreover, people from minority ethnicities are less likely to get diagnosed at all, especially in communities where autism is approached with stigma; as with all minority-related actions, diagnosis takes longer and can be less accurate.

However, I can assure you that you know autistic people, although some might not know they are on the spectrum or might not have a formal diagnosis. Indeed, having worked in IT, I can comfortably say that many of my colleagues were on the spectrum and didn't know it, just as I didn't know that I was until I got diagnosed. And if not for that diagnosis, I would still be living the way I was then: not knowing why I processed the world just a little bit differently and trying to figure out why the world is the way it is.

For some of the people who know me but have not spoken to me about it, my diagnosis will come as a surprise. Yes, I, Jolie, was diagnosed as autistic in my late thirties. My diagnosis came as a result of me undergoing autistic burnout, which meant that I found it more challenging to continue masking or fitting in as I used to. I did not get my autism from the burnout, nor did I develop it later on in life; unbeknownst to me, it had been there all along! But how was it even possible that I could live 37 years with autism and not even know it?

Like many undiagnosed autistics or other minorities or outsiders, I mastered how to fit in with other people through masking –a process we will discuss in detail later on – regardless of how confusing, and sometimes detrimental, that was for me. Luckily, I came from a large and diverse family with many cousins and was fortunate enough to grow up in a country where people, even if stigmatised with many issues, still knew how to treat one another with respect. So, just try to imagine some of the rules I had to learn to abide by after I left my home and moved to more emotionally reserved countries:

> *"Ask your neighbour how they are, but don't wait for (or expect) a response! If they ask you how you are, don't say anything more than 'Fine, thanks' or 'Good, thanks' – never say how you are genuinely feeling, even if you have no clue how you are! And don't forget to smile, even if you just walked out of your best friend's funeral or had a sewing machine fall on your toes! Keep it brief; if you answer honestly, you may be seen as too open, oversharing or even boring. If you like someone, be cold towards them or even mean! Men can swear, but if you are a woman, you are expected to be mild, cute and giggly. Remember the problems that happened when you swore like a pirate in ladies' company or acted too girly at a basketball game, where all your male friends wondered if you were unwell! However, if you are asked if you would like something, don't just answer briefly – make sure you fluff it up with 'Yes please, I would love some of that' because just saying 'Yes' is bad. Be careful to speak to elders in a specific way, but shout from on top of the roof when with friends…unless you are in a church. Then it's all whispers, no giggles and be serious as if you are at a funeral – even if it is a wedding!"*

As you can probably imagine, the diagnosis came as such a huge relief after a lifetime spent thinking that the world was overly complicated or that maybe I was just wrong in every way. Then I realised that the world was designed for the preferences of the neurotypical majority, without any consideration for the needs of the underdiagnosed autistic minority. Now, before you all rush out to pursue a diagnosis or to disclose the diagnosis that you have kept hidden, there are some things that are worth taking into consideration before sharing your autistic status with the world at large.

While there can be many benefits to seeking (or revealing) an autism diagnosis as an adult, it's important to know that it can bring unexpected complications into your life as well. As things start making sense and you begin to mask less, even those close to you will be less familiar with your less masked persona and might not understand the challenges you face in social settings. While this will take time for them to adjust to, there might be a period of people doubting you or your diagnosis. You might be punished for your new way of communicating, and some people might drift away the moment they learn of your diagnosis, even if you continue to mask. If this happens, you need to remember that it's not you, it's them. They might not be very knowledgeable about autism, and what knowledge

5

they do have may be coloured by what they have heard or seen through the media's often exaggerated or inaccurate views on autism. You might also feel a sense of immense loneliness, even when surrounded by other people – not to mention the new biases, gaslighting or microaggressions you may encounter (which is addressed in more detail in Chapter 6). Nevertheless, even with all that said, if I had it to do all over again, would I go back and tell my past self not to get my diagnosis? Absolutely not – I am still glad that I did get it! However, I also do not deny the confusion and loneliness I had (and sometimes still have) to go through after finally learning who I really am and how my brain works after decades of trying to navigate what a neurotypical world has prescribed for me!

Some of those who are on the spectrum will be diagnosed at a young age and given the appropriate support, while others, like me, will fly under the radar. Autistic people can do well with some parts of a structured school environment, such as the tendency towards clear rules (autistic people are great at following rules). Conversely, school can also be a very loud, colourful, messy and confusing place for young people on the spectrum, all of which can affect both their academic performance and their chances of receiving an early diagnosis. One day we might not get the highest grades, and the next we might be top of the class, raising suspicions about our inconsistency. However, that inconsistency might stem from a tendency to perform better on coursework that can be completed at home, without distraction, rather than in a timed 60-minute exam in a room where the invigilator's shoes make a squeaky noise as they walk that keeps us from concentrating or the sound of the clocks ticking feels as loud as our heartbeat and distracts us. Far too often, young people on the spectrum remain under the radar, causing frustration for the teachers, who fail to understand why we can be both excellent and terrible students (sometimes even on the same day), and pain and confusion for the students who are told off for being rude when they have no idea what they have done wrong!

> *"I lived my whole life thinking I was a faulty horse, until I found out that I am not a horse – I am a zebra."*

So, we learn to "fit in". We learn social norms by studying those around us and what we see portrayed in movies and on television and by paying close attention to what gets other people rewarded and avoiding any behaviour contrary to that (e.g., that which leads to us being bullied or mocked). We learn those social norms the same way we learn algebra – the main difference being that with algebra and maths equations, there is only one right answer, whereas, in social contexts, there can be many right (and just as many wrong) answers…answers that can quickly become more complicated when considering different cultural, national, gender-related, generational, event-specific or many other factors!

Whether a person on the spectrum receives plentiful support throughout their childhood or flies completely under the radar, they will meet a new set of challenges when they graduate to the working environment. Tests here tend to come with far greater stakes than mere grades as poor performance now threatens their long-term career goals or immediate livelihoods. Office politics now enter the equation as well – and without a "headteacher" to watch out for them, autistic people are left at the mercy of their work organisation's culture, local or national culture, their supervisors' and coworkers' biases, and a plethora of other rules, both spoken and unspoken. Autistic people might struggle to connect with their coworkers in ways that neurotypical and allistic people take for granted (the term "allistic" refers to people who don't have autism, although they could still be neurodivergent in other ways). We might be less likely to remember to greet you or not engage in small talk before jumping right into a discussion of how to solve a project issue. We might not get your jokes or make enough eye contact with you. Then again, we might make such a masking effort to engage you with eye contact that we end up accidentally overdoing it and staring at you instead!

Misunderstandings like these, along with an overall lack of inclusion, are why more than 80% of autistic people are unemployed or underemployed even when they have the background, skills, qualifications and experience to match or outperform their neurotypical peers. **Those misunderstandings are also why we wrote this book: to transform misunderstanding and ignorance into understanding, acceptance, and awareness and thus**

enable more organisations to tap this hidden talent pool and benefit mutually.

> *"The second time I was not given my promotion, it was because I was a 'fast and detailed speaker and not sharp on the edges'. The third time, it was because I 'spoke too slow and briefly'. Then, I was asked to write out my promotion case in 10,000 words and why I deserved a promotion. When I submitted my resignation instead, I was miraculously given the promotion, along with a 10% salary raise, and asked to not resign. But it was far too late for that as I [had already] signed my next contract. This is a perfect example of ableism."*

A few centuries ago, it would have been unheard of to have a woman working in a position of power; in many places, a black person was not afforded any of the liberties that a fellow white citizen was. Less than a century ago (and still in some countries), those who had a same-gender preference were sent to mental institutes. And unfortunately, until as recently as August 2022, autism was still seen as a mental health condition in the UK. Only then was it formally reclassified to indicate that autism, with all the masking and discrimination that often comes along with it, can lead to mental health issues. This, I suppose, is the same with any form of diversity that is stigmatised and not accepted or included holistically within society. What amazing talent pools would we be missing out on if the world had not changed to become more inclusive? This is the case with autism and other neurodiversities, which represent a valuable talent pool that many organisations are either failing to fully benefit from or missing out on entirely or detrimentally forcing it.

I trust you will enjoy reading this book, that it encourages you to learn more and continue educating yourself through other books and additional sources, and that it brings you better insight, understanding and acceptance.

One final note as we close out this introduction: all of the quotes that you read throughout have come from real people who endured these situations in real life and shared them with us. They have chosen to share their experiences – often with pain and sometimes through tears – in the hope of making the world more open-minded, more accepting, more accessible, and changing the narrative for future generations so they do not have to continue enduring what previous generations have suffered unnecessarily. Please accept those experiences with a great sense of compassion and a minimal sense of judgement; we hope they may prove beneficial in opening the eyes of a colleague, friend or family member who might be facing similar challenges, knowing or unknowingly.

CHAPTER 1

The Medical versus the Social Disability Model

Before we delve into the world of autism, we will need to start by explaining the two types of disability models: the medical model and the social disability model. These are two distinct – and very different – frameworks that are used to understand and address disabilities.

The medical model views disability as a problem caused by a person's physical or mental impairment. It is characterised by a focus on the medical diagnosis and treatment of the individual's condition, with little consideration for the social and environmental factors that may contribute to their experience as a person living with a disability. The medical model emphasises the limitations and deficiencies of the individual and places the burden for treating or managing the condition on the disabled person themselves. Take, for example, the standard approach for treating a condition like diabetes, in which the responsibility for injecting insulin, checking glucose levels and so on fully falls on the person living with diabetes. The medical model takes the position that it is their condition, and therefore their responsibility to manage it properly. It is widely used in clinical settings and is the basis for many disability policies and programmes in countries around the world.

In contrast, the social disability model views disability as a social construct that is also shaped by societal attitudes and environmental barriers rather than just the condition itself. This model recognises that many barriers exist that prevent individuals with disabilities from fully participating in society and emphasises the importance of removing these barriers in order to promote inclusivity and equal opportunities for all individuals. The social model also recognises the diversity of experiences that exist within the disabled community and the importance of valuing and listening to the individual's perspective.

Let's look at an example to explore the differences between these two models. Imagine that a wheelchair user is unable to enter a building because the entrance is located up a long flight of stairs, and there are no ramps or wheelchair-accessible lifts available for their use. Under the medical disability model, society would just stare at them and expect the wheelchair user to find a way to get up the stairs on their own as it is on them to take care of their situation. With the social disability model, on the other hand, society would recognise the environmental barrier preventing the wheelchair user from accessing the building and would provide a ramp or lift to enable them.

Understandably, the medical disability model often leads to stigmatisation and the exclusion of people living with disabilities, while the social disability model has been gaining an increased amount of recognition and acceptance in recent years. It has influenced disability policies and practices in countries around the world, including the United Nations Convention on the Rights of Persons with Disabilities[2], which was adopted in 2006 and based directly on the social disability model. We have the social disability model to thank for the fact that, in the UK, all public places and office buildings of a certain size are legally obliged to provide ramps for wheelchair users.

Unlike some other forms of neurodivergence, autism is not directly medicated, nor are there discrete external accommodations (like wheelchair ramps) that can be easily provided for it. The responsibility for accommodating the condition generally seems to fall on the autistic person themselves. Often, their success will depend on how good they are at masking their autism and how well their mental health resilience functions in terms of dealing with the unique challenges that they face, in addition to the added strain placed upon them by masking and society. This is, unfortunately, a textbook example of the medical disability model at work, wherein the onus for managing the disability fully lies with the individual. It assumes that there is only one right way to develop physiologically or neurologically and that anything that deviates from that norm must be fixed or changed. This approach can work with certain conditions, like diabetes, which can be managed successfully by regulating glucose levels by introducing testing and insulin. However, it does not work with autism – and never will.

We need to shift society away from this medical disability model in its attitudes towards autism and transition into a social disability model. The autistic participant quoted below addresses this need quite clearly, referencing a TED talk he learnt it from:

> "*[The neurodiversity paradigm is an] alternative way of thinking about autism; just like biodiversity creates a healthy and sustainable environment, neurodiversity creates a healthy and sustainable cognitive environment. There are no right or wrong forms of the human brain. Regardless of what kind of brain we have, all people are entitled to full and equal human rights, dignity, and respect. In other words, no more 'But you are less autistic than others' or 'You don't have disabling autism'. Maybe you can't tell by looking at me or others in this room, but we are all disabled too – but not by our autism or ADHD or dyslexia; we are disabled by our environment.*"

We were not all brilliant maths students back in school. However, those of us who struggled with maths were not just kicked out of class and told never to study it again, that we were terrible at it, and it was our problem to figure out on our own. We were either taught using different methods or given extra support and still managed to progress in school and learn basic multiplication or division as a result. There is no one way of thinking; neurodiversity is needed as much as biodiversity is for balance and cognitive diversity - a catalyst for innovation.

A social disability model would work wonders to enable neurodivergent people even if it were only partly applied within workplaces. Unfortunately, many workplaces simply refuse to adopt it for autism – or other neurodiversities – because they are hidden disabilities and due to the fear of change. This is not a problem that is unique to autism – according to the latest statistics compiled by the UK Parliament (Jan 2023), 70-80% of all disabilities within the UK are actually hidden/invisible disabilities[3]! Take a minute to consider the following neurodivergent employee's experience with their performance review:

"'Weird...too talkative...does not say good morning... speaks loudly...does not respond or act as cool as others, and sometimes speaks with a different tone or needs more time to process.' It is not okay to ask non-fluent English-speaking colleagues to 'change' their accent, or to tell a female colleague to only come to work with full makeup; but

*it seems to be okay to tell masking autistics they are not masking well enough – to speak lower, or not interrupt, or to say certain things in a certain way. People need to hear **what** we say rather than **how** we say it – the same way we process what everyone else says!"*

CHAPTER 2

Some Overdue Definitions

When it comes to definitions, the aim of this book is to give you as close as possible to a first-hand understanding rather than a rigid textbook definition. That said, it is important to start with a high-level definition of the term neurodiversity; I promise this will be one of only very few textbook definitions I will take you through over the course of this book!

The term neurodiversity was coined by sociologist Judy Singer in 1998 and refers to cognitive and brain diversity. Singer's work[4] [5] helped popularise the idea that human cognitive variation and functions – e.g., reading social cues, attention, creativity, pattern detection, learning and sensory responses, etc. – are similar to biodiversity and therefore needed in society as a whole. In other words, differences in the way people's brains work make the world a better place. Singer's research, and that of others like Harvey Blume and Thomas Armstrong[6], contributed immensely to the backbone of minority group policies as well as the perception of social versus medical inclusion models. It also inspired Laura Tisonicik to create the term neurotypical, which frames the neurologically typical as being the opposite of the neurodivergent. Neurotypical is different from people who are allistic – a term that refers to those who are not on the spectrum but who could be either neurodivergent or neurotypical. Over time, the term neurodiversity has come to serve as an umbrella term covering autism, ADHD, dyslexia, dyspraxia, OCD, dyscalculia and other cognitive diversities. While we will be exploring other neurodiversities in future books, this book focuses specifically on autism due to our first-hand experience of the subject.

The fact that you are reading this book means that you are privileged to know at least one or more people who are on the spectrum. If you know more than one, you will no doubt agree that they act very differently from one another

- as the saying goes: meeting one autistic person means you only met *one* autistic person!

Though autism is currently being extensively researched, what we know about it scientifically is still not very clear. Unfortunately, most of the existing research funding tends to go towards "Why does autism exist?" studies rather than projects that would more directly benefit people on the spectrum. Some have tried to link it to vaccines, others have tried to link it to trauma (even pre-birth trauma), but no conclusive origin has been confirmed. However, most researchers agree that autism is not determined by a single gene but by as many as 200–400 genes; some recent research has claimed it might even involve thousands of genes and their variations! The only thing that *is* clear is that it is not as simple as having an "on or off" gene that either means "yes, you have autism" or "no, you are neurotypical." The complexity surrounding the genetics causing autism is why we see such a broad spectrum, and why some people might have other neurodiversities or conditions coexisting alongside their autism.

Furthermore, it is important to mention that there are also many different types of autism, including Asperger's syndrome, Rett syndrome, childhood disintegrative disorder, Kanner's syndrome and pervasive developmental disorder. In this book, we will focus on the type of autism most commonly found at work, which is Asperger's syndrome.

Politics

We all knew it had to come up sooner or later, so let's get the politics out of the way!

For the sake of political correctness, the term "Asperger's" is used much less than it used to be as it was coined by Hans Asperger, who is believed to have been linked with the Nazis. Now, people tend to refer to Asperger's under the general umbrella of autism spectrum disorder (ASD), though some people who are on the spectrum take issue with that term. They reason that autism is not a disorder and see that name as not enabling them as it is their environment that disables them and not the autism itself. So, the term "ASD" is currently evolving to either "AS (autism spectrum) person" or "person on the autism spectrum". Some people from the AS community still prefer to use the term "Asperger's" or might also refer to themselves as "Aspies", "atypical", "Aspergian" (as Elon Musk calls himself) or "autistic".

We should also explain that the term "autistic" is frowned upon by professionals in the field, who prefer to use person-first language to emphasise the person rather than the condition, disorder or disability; that is why professionals promote the use of phrases like "person with autism" or "a person on the AS" rather than "autistic". The goal of person-first language is to reduce stereotyping and discrimination by emphasising the person's individuality rather than their condition. However, most of the autism community (which includes both those with autism and their families) prefers to use identity-first language. 87% of those on the spectrum who participated in one US-based study preferred to use identity-first language like "autistic". They emphasised that it allowed them to embrace all the aspects of their identity, unlike the person-first language (person with autism) preferred by professionals[7].

No two people on the spectrum are the same; however, no one should be reduced to "high-functioning" (used to refer to Asperger's or those with no obvious intellectual difficulties) or "low-functioning" stereotypes either. All those who are on the spectrum may have certain struggles or the same amount of autism, but due to sensitivities, variations, exposures and masking, their conditions may appear different to those looking in. The "high-functioning/low-functioning" labels continued to be used until recently even by professionals; however, most are now moving away from that kind of binary classification towards the use of levels 1, 2 and 3 to describe different presentations of autism.

Level 1, also referred to as "requiring support", can be considered either the "least severe" level of autism or the level with the highest masking ability. These are people who have some difficulties in social interactions or in areas that masking might not generally cover. While this category would be where most of our work colleagues can be found, they are usually the hardest to diagnose and the worst hit by the impact of masking; they may struggle more with mental health as well due to a lack of support and the strain of over-masking.

Level 2, also referred to as "requiring substantial support", tends to feature more limited social interactions and narrow special interests. People with level 2 autism may display frequent restricted repetitive behaviours and, in many cases, need support addressing their wants and needs as they may not be able to communicate them; if they can, it is normally with limited words or the assistance of technological aids.

Level 3, also referred to as "requiring very substantial support", is considered the most severe level of the autism spectrum. Most level 3 individuals have severe difficulties in verbal and non-verbal social communication and may experience restrictive and repetitive behaviour even more frequently than people at level 2. This impacts their ability to be independent and can severely affect their social interactions, sometimes causing aggression or making them the victims of aggression. Level 3 individuals need the most support addressing their wants and needs as they may not be able to communicate them; if they can, it might be with a very limited vocabulary or using technological aids. People with level 3 autism experience severe distress and difficulty with routine changes, focus changes, or unexpected actions and use the least masking of the three levels.

Unfortunately, there have been a lot of stereotypes that have worked to misguide the general public's perception of autism. It is ironic that most of the TV shows, movies and media depicting autism are created by people who are not autistic and have neither a lived experience with autism nor a true understanding of what autism really is. This has led to a very distorted public understanding of autism, even when these non-autistic writers and creators are trying to be inclusive. For example, the tendency to emphasise the savant traits associated with autistic people in media portrayals of autism puts pressure on those who do not have the savant syndrome to have to explain why they aren't, in fact, "just like Sheldon Cooper or the Good Doctor". Neither is it helpful to have a neurotypical person, when dealing with an autistic person for the first time, make it a point to "watch out" for when they have a meltdown or anticipate difficulty in communication before they start conversing. If anything, the well-meaning neurotypical is likelier to lead them into one by overloading them with a series of probing questions – in many cases because a TV show they watched "confirmed" that autistic people do not feel as much as non-autistic people. For many individuals, this kind of performative "helpfulness" is even becoming a trend – and for many organisations, it is becoming a new area in which to show off how cutting edge they are with their "commitment to diversity and inclusion". Though well-intentioned, these inaccurate media portrayals of autism (and the misguided sense of "helpfulness" they inspire) are disastrous for people who really are autistic and are forced to endure a lot of gaslighting as a result. No autistic person should ever have to listen to someone tell them, "No way you are autistic – I just watched a programme about it", but that still happens all the time. The misuse of normalising language can also be harmful:

> *"Saying, 'everybody is a bit autistic' is the same as confusing occasional anxiousness for having an anxiety disorder that cripples your options, privileges and everyday life."*

We do not tell someone in a wheelchair that "We all like to sit down now and again" or a blind person that "I'm so blind, I couldn't see you with all these people around" – no! Just…no. It is harmful, it is inhumane, and it completely minimises the struggles that person lives with every day of their life.

Phew! Okay – now that we have got the politics out of the way, let us get back to business!

CHAPTER 3

So, What Is Autism and What Does it Feel Like?

An Intro to Autism

Autism is more than a set of external traits; since autism has been known, autistic traits have always been described from the outside, i.e., as seen or experienced by allistic people. Only looking at autism from the outside means that the richest and most important, internal parts of the autistic experience are missed. When the "external view" describes autism as "deficits in social and emotional exchanges", that is what the world sees, and it encourages people to only focus on the external traits of a person who is overwhelmed with their surroundings and might be traumatised or struggling to cope with unwritten or unspoken norms. So, instead of discussing "adverse reactions or extreme sensitivity to sensory stimuli", how about we look at what it feels like for someone on the spectrum and how that may trigger that external view?

As discussed, no two people on the spectrum will be the same, based on genetics and the fact that there are different types of autism. While one person on the spectrum might not talk at all, with another, it might be difficult to get them to stop talking! While one might struggle with light, another might find it so stimulating that they have to be told not to look at it, even though many autistic people perceive light to be much brighter than their allistic peers do.

> *"Did you know that light is perceived as up to 40% brighter for autistic people? Even worse is how they flicker – yes, we can see the frequency of it! Luckily, I don't have epilepsy, as that's how clearly we can see the flickering. While blue glasses may help some, they do not eliminate the headaches and eye aches that come from the constant flickering, nor do they stop the sound of the electric currents buzzing. No wonder I feel exhausted whenever I'm in the office with all those lights! I can switch some of them off, but my colleagues*

> *prefer a 'well-lit' work environment, so I try to sit next to the window to balance things out with natural light instead."*

The same goes with noise.

> *"Most kids fell asleep to the sound of white noise. Meanwhile, I was kept wide awake by any noise! Perfume is highly sought after and some people will pay a lot of money for it; but for me, the smell of perfume can be as offensive as the smell of coffee or someone who has not showered in days!"*

Even with all these variations, one thing that all AS individuals have in common is a hyper or hypo sensitivity to the world around them. The quote below might sound like an exaggeration or an overreaction to a neurotypical person – but it will make a lot more sense once we explain just how debilitating these sensitivities can be!

> *"I had to quit a job because my manager had terrible coffee breath. She was a brilliant leader, but I had to move within the firm to avoid smelling that breath every day when she was in close proximity to me. It didn't help that she had five to seven coffees throughout the day."*

In the previous chapter, we explained what it means to be on the spectrum genetically speaking; but what does it actually *feel* like for someone who is on the spectrum?

Let's try to visualise what it's like inside the mind of an autistic person using a simple analogy: think of the brain as having many pigeonholes – one for each sense. There's a pigeonhole for sight, a pigeonhole for smell, one for touch, and so on.

Figure 1: Neurotypical: One message per sense

When a neurotypical person sees something, that signal will be sent to the sight pigeonhole in their brain. If they smell something, that signal will be sent directly to their smell pigeonhole. The paths these signals take (as far as this analogy goes, at least), travel in a straight line from the input point right to the particular pigeonhole where the brain processes that kind of stimulus – a nice, clear, straightforward process. Easy-peasy, right?

Well, when a person with autism sees something, that signal bounces all over their senses' pigeonholes, numerous times and extensively. And what if they should happen to smell something at the same time? Now all their pigeonholes will be bombarded by a combination of sight and smell signals, all getting tossed about, in numerous quantities, simultaneously. Imagine trying to carry on a conversation with 15 people who are all speaking to you at the same time and responding to each one of them is a priority; now, multiply that a few times. Not fun, right? Not fun at all!

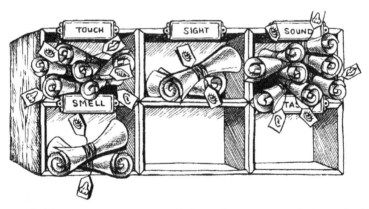

Figure 2: Numerous message rolls inundating senses' pigeonholes

This is where we get the terms sensory overwhelm or sensory overload from. It's also why we get certain traits associated with autism, such as avoiding eye contact while focusing on what someone else is saying, loud places, strong lights, strong smells (both good and bad, depending on a person's sensitivities), public transport, and so on. These sensitivities are also the reason why those on the AS often notice things that others might overlook and can be very good with things like pattern recognition or avoiding unconscious biases. While those aspects of AS sensitivities can be seen as positive traits, such sensitivities can also be a disaster – especially if an autistic person is using more than one sense at the same time. Imagine what it's like for an AS person taking a public transport ride to work where the lights are strong, the train makes loud noises and other commuters are sipping coffees while either lacking in basic hygiene or drenched in perfumes. Then imagine what it's like to walk straight from that train ride into an office building, where the AS person is expected to maintain eye contact while they are being spoken to in a conversation that is taking place inside a brightly lit room, that is next to a road with loud traffic, while phones are ringing, keyboards are clacking and there are a dozen other conversations all taking place within earshot – excruciating to say the least!

Just to make things even more complex, many people on the spectrum are not very good at understanding or describing how they feel emotionally (or benchmarking it towards what is considered the norm in the neurotypical world we live in). This can be referred to as alexithymia, i.e., difficulty with identifying or understanding or describing feelings. Neurologically, this is linked to a person's interoception, which is the sense that allows us to perceive physical sensations (like hunger, tiredness) and how these relate to our feelings or mood. While some still believe the harmful stereotype that autistic people lack empathy, that is simply not true; if anything, current research is proving it might be the exact opposite, with many AS people struggling with overwhelm and anxiety due to hyper-empathy. Those on the spectrum commiserate and can be overly empathetic – they just may not know how to show it in a "typical" or neurotypically accepted way.

"We are great empaths; we absorb the feelings of those around us, but we do not always know how to respond the way they (or society) expect. That doesn't mean we do not feel their pain, or suffering, or joy. Even worse is when we try to connect by saying that we've had a similar experience – when we bare our heart to show the person that we understand part of their pain – and they think that we are competing with them!"

The same has been proven true with pain; a recent pain perception study from Tel Aviv University[8] found that autistic people experience pain at a higher intensity than the general population and are less adaptable to the sensation.

"I laid on the bed for two days crying in agony; when my flatmate arrived home from her travels and realised that my calf was bigger than my thigh, she thought it was an infection and marched me to hospital. Both she and the doctor were shocked to realise I had limped to hospital with a broken tibia after surviving two days with it! His first question was if I was on any illegal drugs, but I assured him that I was not. He then asked how painful it was on a scale of 1-10. I answered, 'Six', to which he asked, 'Why six and not ten?' I explained that ten would probably be giving birth (also known as breaking 200 bones at the same time), nine might be the pain from a heart attack, eight could be a shattered neck or spine, seven a kidney or gallbladder stone, so I had *no right to claim a ten! He continued, asking me why did I not go sooner as he was examining how bad the X-ray looked. I explained that I hadn't come earlier because I thought it would get better, there was a huge pressure on the health system, and the strong lights in the hospital made me feel worse than the idea of tolerating the pain in my leg on my own. His next question still haunts me till this day; he asked why I was not screaming in agony. All I knew was that I was in pain and needed to focus on me and how I felt – I simply didn't know I was autistic then, nor did I have my mask on to fit society's expectations while I was in agony. I imploded to preserve my energy to deal with the pain instead of verbally and vocally exploding. So, I asked him, 'Will you treat me if I start screaming? And do you prefer high-pitched, non-frequent screams, or do you prefer long-term wailing?' The doctor fixed up my cast and gave me the crutches to get rid of me. He probably thought I was being rude or sarcastic, but I was genuinely asking! I wasn't sure how I needed to mask and 'act' as a neurotypical person would in such a situation to get the right (and prompt) response."*

Managing health generally can be a complicated challenge for some autistic people due to struggles with executive functioning; even logging in to get a repeat prescription or to take care of the administrative side of booking an appointment can be disabling for some. Also, the whole "you explain everything you're feeling, then we'll fix you up and send you on your way in ten minutes" aspect of modern medicine can be a challenge for some AS people who struggle with interoception, are more detailed in their responses, or get anxious when they are rushed. And that's still excluding the harsh lights and smells that accompany most medical clinics and the unspoken rules and expectations that still need to be navigated socially.

"At the age of five years old, I could discuss sustainability issues and politics with recognised politicians. By the time I was in Grade 6 (11 years old), I could do college-level biology exams and study it with my brother. I finished university at the age of 19 and started and sold two successful businesses, but I packed my bag and prepared to go to jail when I received my first council tax reminder as I had not paid it and did not know how to and the admin of it all seemed impossible. I packed my bags and called my friends to say I'm heading to jail as the letter threatened me of court. A friend took my phone, called the county council, and set up a direct debit with my card, and I didn't need to go to court or to jail – I happily unpacked my bags! I still find it very distressing when I have to do admin things like fill in forms."

A common (and frustrating) question that autistic people often get asked is some variation of "How can someone with such a good academic background / so many degrees / who is so capable in other areas not be able to do something so simple?" Well, I mentioned above how I was gifted in certain areas as a child yet struggled badly in others. Does that sound familiar? Or maybe a bright child getting into trouble or being brutally honest to a troublesome degree? Well, these things can all be attributed to what is known as a "spiky profile"[9].

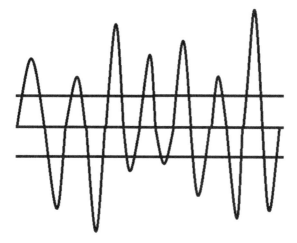

Figure 3: Cognitive abilities of a spiky profile

The straight lines represent neurotypical people's cognitive ability – their strengths, abilities, intellectual quotient (IQ), emotional quotient (EQ) and so on; the oscillations represent someone on the spectrum. They can be brilliant in certain areas but way below the expected average in others.

> *"For me, the peaks showed as me discussing world politics and sustainability as a toddler, or knowing Grade 11 biology while I was still in Grade 5. But the deep valleys are also me practically losing the will to live if something wool touches me, or packing my bags to go to jail when all that was needed was a phone call and the payment of a small bill I didn't manage to send in, or me being too factual/ honest/ literal to the point that it might offend others."*

One term that we have already referred to, and which we will be frequently mentioning from this point forward, is masking, which is something that goes hand in hand with autism. This definition, inspired by the National Autistic Society, perfectly captures what masking is:

> *"Masking is when autistic people suppress certain behaviours that they find soothing but that others think are 'weird', such as stimming or intense interests. It can also mean mimicking the behaviour of those around them (such as copying non-verbal behaviours) and developing complex social scripts to get by in social situations. Over time, we may become more aware of our own masking, but it often*

begins as an unconscious response to social trauma before we even grasp our differences."

The ability to mask is why many autistic people do not get their diagnoses, remain under the radar, or "don't look autistic" to neurotypical people, whatever that means (even though we have never figured out how people saying things like this think they can see how other people's brains work, it is still a common statement made to many autistic people regardless of how severely they are affected by their environments or how well they mask). Masking can include forcing blinks at set time intervals, forcing eye contact, exaggerated body or facial expressions, changing tone of voice, and many other behaviours.

"The strategy of masking shows just how clever and resourceful our minds are at finding ways of coping. It can even be useful at some particularly stressful points in our lives, like during job interviews. – [National Autistic Society].

[Masking] can also be used to stop bullying or other negative outcomes of sticking out. I experience lights as 40% brighter than what most people experience, I can hear even the slightest of sounds as loudly as the person who is talking

> *to me – but I hide it and smile as if nothing is happening other than the person talking. I might even muster the effort for eye contact (i.e., even more masking)."*

The work of Dr Amy Pearson and Kieran Rose[10] portrays masking as, at its core, a form of trauma response. It is a way of telling the aggressor – whether they are a bully, an interviewer or a friend we don't want to lose – that we are who they want us to be and will remain so as long as they don't leave or harm us. To satisfy those around us, we take on a new identity or many; this is also common in other minorities or non-homogenous groups when people seek to acquire a sense of belonging and fit within the norm. For AS people, this masking process starts from a very young age. Unlike other conditions which can be medicated or accommodated in other ways (such as pills for ADHD or a hearing aid for those who can't hear), masking is the only way some autistic people feel they can be included or accepted – even by their closest friends and family.

Imagine being on a TV show and being your best self – using perfect conversational scripts and accompanying gestures. Now imagine having to do that all day, every day, for life. Even when you are not in the right physical or mental state for it or you need your brain power to work on something complex. It is, quite frankly, exhausting. Unfortunately, it is also one of the main causes of autistic burnout and mental health depletion in autistic people.

> *"Remember the scene in [the movie] 'X-Men: First Class' where Mystique is working out in her human form and struggling, and then Magneto takes the weight from her and tells her that if she's using half her concentration to look normal, then she's only using half of her concentration in whatever else she does? That's exactly how much strain masking has; it is **exhausting** to always be masking. It is not sustainable or healthy to constantly mask, but it is also not a choice – not to us – as the moment we relax our mask, we immediately regret it."*

While we are here, let's explain what stimming, or self-stimulatory behaviour, is: stimming is a repetitive movement (such as rocking, humming or fidgeting with a toy) that helps an autistic person regulate their sensory experiences, reduce anxiety, control their sensory input or feel a sense of familiarity and comfort. While stimming can be beneficial for individuals with autism, it is often stigmatised or misunderstood by others. It is important to recognise that stimming is a valid and vital coping mechanism for many autistic individuals and attempts to discourage or eliminate it can be harmful[11]. Stimming seems to generally be associated only with autistic people, though I have witnessed neurotypical people do it without it being labelled as stimming. As autistic people have to deal with more sensory inputs and overwhelm from their surroundings, along with other stresses that can be more than what a neurotypical person typically deals with stress-wise, they may reach the point where they need to stim much faster and do it without witnessing social norms. When a neurotypical person is stressed, they may move their foot or knee repetitively, pace up and down the corridor of their office building, or even just twiddle their thumbs to release some of the pressure or stress they are facing. We do not ask them to stop any of these coping mechanisms, nor do we ask someone in a wheelchair to get up and walk. Yet it is somehow okay to tell autistic kids and adults to stop or be ashamed about their stimming, even though it is a harmless way for them to find that sense of calm or familiarity in a hectic, loud and fast world that was not designed with any of their needs in mind.

> *"I kept playing the same song over and over again. After hearing it for about two hours, my partner asked if I was okay, and that's when I realised that it was what was giving me the sense of familiarity and safety that I needed to ground myself. Yoga, meditation, all those things don't seem to work for me. Listening to the same song repetitively or moving my feet in a wave motion grounds me better."*

Of course, it's important to keep in mind that not all autistic people stim. Many have also learnt how to mask it, even if that comes at a high cost for their mental health.

Meltdowns – which we will discuss further in the myth-busting chapter that follows this one – are characterised by a loss of control over one's emotions and often result in behaviours such as crying, screaming or lashing out. Though they are often confused for one another, meltdowns are very different from burnout, which is a state of physical, emotional and mental exhaustion that results from masking, chronic stress and overwhelm over an extended period. It also takes longer to recover from burnout than a meltdown. Nevertheless, despite their differences, both burnout and meltdowns can be absolutely debilitating for autistic people and can seriously interfere with their daily functioning. In many ways, autistic burnout is similar to other forms of burnout, such as that resulting from stress or overwork; it is also unique in several aspects as autistic burnout can result in an AS person losing certain abilities or skills that they had previously mastered.

> "I used to paint and sketch beautifully; the colours or shape of the sketch would be perfectly clear in my mind before I carefully transferred them to paper or porcelain. I was also brilliant with my choice of words, always able to express myself beautifully. But ever since I had my autistic burnout, I lost those abilities. I can barely remember half the vocabulary I once knew –words run away from me, and when I hold a pencil or a paintbrush, it is as if my hand and my brain speak very different languages and can no longer communicate. At first, I was actually suspected of having suffered a stroke or early-onset Alzheimer's. It was only after a doctor who had seen this before mentioned the possibility of autistic burnout and I was checked for autism then we realised that was what was happening to me. I miss painting and sketching. I miss being able to use many words to indulge the experiences I am trying to portray – but alas, I am not sure if I will again, or when it will happen."

Some Strengths and Challenges: Common Traits Associated with Autism

Autism is often characterised in terms of deficits or challenges. While such characterisations might be true for some, for others, there can be many positive traits associated with autism. While people on the autism spectrum do not all share the same formative experiences or traits, these are some traits that are often associated with those on the spectrum at the workplace:

- Attention to detail and accuracy: individuals with autism often have strong attention to detail and may be able to notice and remember things that others overlook[12].

- Enhanced pattern detection and visual learning.

- Good long-term (but *not* short-term/working) memory and recall.

- Highly observational and good with research.

- Original thinking: autistic individuals may think in unique and creative ways, approaching problems and tasks from unconventional directions and finding solutions others might not have thought of[13].

- Honesty: autistic individuals may have a tendency to be honest, to the point where they may even struggle to lie. Their unmasked and culturally influenced communication style is direct, without the use of social niceties, pleasantries, or euphemisms[14].

- Strong sense of justice and less prone to unconscious bias.

- Less prone to being judgemental.

- Loyalty: autistic individuals form strong and lasting bonds with those they care about, demonstrating a strong sense of loyalty and commitment[15]. This is shown in their lower turnover rate with their employers; when things get tough, autistic people are less likely to get going!

- Deep focus, concentration and perseverance: autistic individuals may have a strong ability to focus on tasks and a greater ability to persevere in the face of challenges[16].

Some recent research conducted at JP Morgan suggested that autistic employees were as much as 48% faster and 92% more productive than their neurotypical colleagues. This may be attributed to monotropism, a cognitive style associated with autism that gives autistic individuals an increased ability to focus on certain tasks and concentrate for an extended period of time. This cognitive style may be what causes some individuals with autism to develop such in-depth knowledge and expertise within their areas of interest, which can be valuable in many professions; however, it may also be the reason why it can be challenging (and highly depleting) for some autistic individuals to switch between tasks.

These positive traits are just a few examples of some of the strengths that autistic individuals can bring to the workplace and the greater world at large. By recognising and building upon these strengths, we can include, support and empower individuals with autism to succeed within the workplace while benefiting from their unique capabilities.

Nevertheless, as with all areas of life, there are also some traits or challenges faced by autistic individuals that can impact their daily life, causing them to struggle or preventing them from achieving their full potential. These challenges, or the way they are responded to, can lead to people on the spectrum feeling unwelcomed or unaccepted by others. Again, please remember that not all autistic people are the same, so not all AS individuals will have these traits or be impacted by them in the same ways. Some may be very good at masking them, or simply display these traits in other ways. Such traits could include the following:

- **Hyper or hypo sensory sensitivities**: many individuals with autism have sensory sensitivities, which can lead to discomfort or distress in response to certain stimuli, such as loud noises or bright lights[17]. (Remember the pigeonhole analogy we made a few sections back?)

- **Social communication differences**: individuals with autism may experience difficulty with non-inclusive social communication, including challenges with eye contact which can manifest as either avoidance of eye contact or a tendency towards staring-it is a spectrum, after all! Others might struggle to understand social cues and comprehend the conventional back-and-forth nature of conversation. (This might not be as much of an issue if the person has grown up in a multicultural environment where there are different accepted norms surrounding communication styles).

- **Other communication differences**, such as a tendency for being literal and difficulties understanding body language, proximity and tone or volume of voice during conversations.

- **Executive functioning challenges**, which may impact an individual's ability to plan, organise, initiate and complete paperwork or simple life tasks (e.g., the laundry or paying bills); such challenges can also have a direct effect on AS individuals' academic or social lives[18].

- **Restricted or focused interests and repetitive behaviours**: these have already been discussed as a potential strength but can also create challenges for people on the spectrum, especially when their heightened focus or routine interferes with social interactions and other daily activities.

- **Difficulty with change and transition**: this can cause anxiety and heightened stress and lead to meltdowns or shutdowns.

- **Overwhelming emotions and heightened sensitivity**, which can lead to shutdown, meltdown, selective mutism and hypo reactivity.

- **Stimming, rocking or other familiar repetitive movements**: while these are helpful for the person on the spectrum, they are often not accepted or welcomed in less inclusive environments.

- **Difficulties with proprioception**, including body positioning or a tendency towards clumsiness: while this may be related to a different neurodiversity known as dyspraxia, many people on the spectrum who do not have dyspraxia still approximate objects or people as being much closer than they are in reality and may have some of the proprioception mentioned above.

- **Avoiding sensory flooding experiences**: while this sounds like it should be a basic right, it is not something that can easily be avoided as a simple trip to the grocery store often involves flooding the autistic person's senses with lights, noises and cool and warm sensations, along with all the other humans who bring along with them their assorted smells, noises and movements.

- **Detailed processing**: another trait that can be viewed as a positive in some circumstances and as a negative in others; overthinking and attention to detail are two things that simply go hand in hand with autism.

- **Atypical expressions**: while some are great at masking, learning social norms like they would algebra or the grammatical use of the comma, others struggle more in this aspect. Autistic people try to mask by displaying facial expressions or gestures that they believe will be appropriate to the social situation. Sometimes these expressions can come off as exaggerated or incorrect due to subpar masking or not remembering which expression or mask to apply in that particular situation!

AUTISTIC & SMASHING IT

As discussed previously, AS individuals may struggle with interoception (including thirst, hunger or emotional awareness).

These challenges can vary widely in their severity and impact, and it is important to recognise that each autistic individual will have their own unique strengths, challenges, preferences and adjustments when it comes to dealing with them.

CHAPTER 4

Busting Some Common Myths and Misunderstandings

We know that some of you might be thinking, "Wow, does this topic really deserve a whole chapter?" And the answer to that is a hearty, "Yes! Yes, it absolutely does!"

> *"No one believed my autism diagnosis when I got it at 37 years of age! Everyone said, 'Really? But you are a social butterfly', or 'But you're the soul of the party' or 'You always come up with the best social plans.' They didn't realise that I gained so much of my comfort from planning events that involved theatre, dancing and activities because they did not require much talking but more watching or moving to loud music. It was always such a nightmare though when we would be dancing and someone would decide to have an in-depth conversation."*

Meltdowns

We already discussed stimming and how neurotypical people do it, just not as much as autistic people (and without the same kind of stigma attached). Well, a similar thing happens with meltdowns, so we think it is important to talk about what meltdowns are and how they happen to both autistic AND neurotypical people. Can you think back to when a friend or colleague was going through a crisis in their life – maybe a divorce or an unexpected financial loss? Can you remember how that person who was overwhelmed with stress and had no obvious solution or immediate reason to hope started panicking? Maybe they started plodding around the room, or shouting at those around them, or punching a wall or a desk? (Those are all examples I personally witnessed take place in real life from neurotypical people, by the way). Well, autistic people do the same whenever they feel an overwhelming amount of stress! It is just that autistic people are exposed to more pressures and stresses and the level or type of stress can be quite different from what overwhelms a neurotypical person due to the constant strain of their hyper or hypo sensitivities. It might only take a work event in a loud pub to get a person on the spectrum to that stage of overwhelm or something as simple as a "serious talk" with a teacher or a loud and overstimulating car or public transport ride. These stress levels are also heavily affected by the fact that an autistic person's surroundings do not cater to the needs of their hidden disability. As per the extract quoted below, we can see that in some situations an autistic person can actually be more resilient and remain more clearly focused on seeking a solution than their neurotypical colleagues might be:

> "While everyone was panicking and running around, I was calmly ensuring that everything was in place and ready in case we needed to run for our lives. The neurotypicals around me were crying and devastated. But because there was no electricity or harsh lights to distract me, I remained in a state of calm while surrounded by adults who were freaking out and having meltdowns. I didn't shame anyone then, nor do I shame colleagues now when they have their worries and meltdowns; but somehow, it still seems normal for others to shame or belittle my concerns instead of asking if I'm okay, or just leaving me alone to deal with the exhaustion and shame of having had a meltdown."

Overthinking and Oversharing

It seems to be a new fad to tell people not to "overthink" – well, here's some news for you: overthinking and autism are directly linked! Oversharing too, while we are at it! We've already discussed how the autistic brain processes details differently from the neurotypical brain and how that actually IS a strength for those who are on the spectrum. So, when you tell someone on the spectrum not to overthink, in effect it is like you are telling them not to think at all – another unspoken rule that autistic people are expected to know intuitively! Oversharing can be easier to resolve, as you can always ask an autistic individual to briefly tell you about this, that or the other thing. Remember, an autistic person is not oversharing or overthinking because they *want* to agonise or torture you; they overshare because they either don't know or struggle to "read" the norms of how much detail it is appropriate to go into or how genuine you actually are about wanting to know the answer (i.e., do you REALLY want to know more about their day or were you just asking to be polite?) And being as eager as they are to assist, an autistic person's desire to not leave out any information you might find useful leads them to overshare.

> *"The till lady at the supermarket asked me, 'How are you?' And I genuinely replied, 'Not great – I have my period, I feel like a monster is ravaging and munching my ovaries, my back hurts really badly, and I have to carry my child who doesn't want to walk anymore, yet I still have to do the shopping as my partner is playing video games and feeling sorry for himself because he has a runny nose.' The till lady was gobsmacked by my response – I guess she just expected a 'Fine, thank you' – and I was mortified as I realised that my response was not what she was expecting and rather traumatising."*

Conversational Norms

Autistic individuals may experience challenges with transitioning between different topics during a conversation. One of the difficulties they have with social cues is recognising the signalling that indicates the end of one topic or the beginning of a new one. This can result in everything from abrupt topic changes to difficulty initiating a new topic to interjecting topics that come off as random or off base. It can also result in an AS person waiting so quietly or patiently for their turn to speak that they end up not sharing their idea at all or sharing it too quickly or in a way that neurotypicals might not understand or appreciate, even if the content of the idea itself is actually brilliant. This can lead to a mismatch in communication styles and difficulties in maintaining social relationships, which in turn leaves the autistic person feeling more excluded and unappreciated, causing them to withdraw even more / interact less, making it even harder for them to maintain social relationships. It's an ugly cycle, and it can be very difficult for the autistic person to break out of it. In addition, autistic individuals may struggle with non-factual or non-literal language, such as idioms or metaphors (e.g., "no room to swing a cat", "he's an early bird", etc.) unless they have been explicitly taught or exposed to them[19]. This can result in misunderstandings or confusion when communicating with neurotypical individuals who frequently use these types of language. These sorts of difficulties with idioms and figurative language can also be confusing for people from different cultures; it's interesting to note how quickly the misunderstanding of an idiom can be laughed off when it's a person from another culture, yet an autistic person suffering from the same misunderstanding can be treated with a far lesser degree of tolerance or compassion when they are the one who's confused!

Furthermore, autistic individuals may have difficulty with social reciprocity/mutuality, which can include asking questions and taking an interest in others during conversations[20]. They may talk about their own interests or ideas without prompting or without asking the other person about their interests or perspectives as they expect the other person to simply respond by talking about themselves. Or, after someone has shared a story about their experience, an autistic individual might respond by telling them about a similar experience they had themselves or that someone else they know had encountered. They are not doing this to disregard the experience they were just told about; this is the autistic person's way of affirming that they care and understand what the other person has gone through. The differences in these communication styles can lead to exclusion, a lack of engagement or understanding, and, in some cases, even anger, bullying or violence towards the autistic individual.

Tone of Voice

Autistic individuals may face challenges when it comes to regulating the volume and tone of their voice due to sensory overload; they can find it difficult to determine the appropriate volume level in a given environment, especially when there are many other background noises affecting their abilities to both hear and concentrate. Additionally, the social norms surrounding voice volume or tone can be difficult for autistic people to decipher, leading to misunderstandings. While some situations call for a softer tone, others require a louder voice to be heard over all the other environmental stimuli; this may lead to the autistic person's intentions or emotions being misinterpreted or otherwise "lost in translation". Autistic individuals may also have a different tone of voice – often described as monotone – or may emphasise different sounds or parts of words than a neurotypical person. Unfortunately, these differences can often be mistaken for boredom or rudeness by neurotypicals who prioritise tone over content. In an effort to mask their autism, some individuals may try to mimic the speech patterns of neurotypicals – perhaps people they know or characters from television shows or movies whom they perceive as being socially adept. This can lead to over-exaggeration, misunderstood sarcasm or the neurotypical person thinking that they are being mocked. Another challenge AS people face in this arena is difficulty interpreting neurotypical tones of voice, which often leads to missed social cues or misunderstandings. Ultimately, it is important to focus on the content of what an autistic individual is saying rather than how they say it.

> *"I was so excited that it was my first football match. It was a bit overwhelming as there were so many people, noises and lights, and everybody was shouting; but I was determined to enjoy my date and the match! During the halftime, my date asked if I was having fun, and I shouted, "YES!" back. He looked at me very awkwardly and continued sipping his drink. He then asked if I was having a good time, and I shouted, "YES!" again. He then got angry and asked why I was being ungrateful and mean to him when he was trying his best to accommodate me. Apparently, he was upset that I was shouting, and regardless of the fact that everybody else who was around us was also shouting, I shouldn't have shouted as I was on a date, and it is only appropriate to use a soft speaking voice during dates – regardless of practicality."*

The Intimacy of Eye Contact

Autistic individuals may experience overwhelm and overstimulation when making eye contact. As we explained earlier with our pigeonhole analogy, making eye contact can be an unpleasant or difficult masking experience for some autistic individuals. This might mean that there will hardly be any eye contact made, or there might be full-on staring with a lack of blinking. With the pigeonhole analogy kept in mind, it should be taken as a compliment when an autistic child or adult is not making eye contact with a speaker as it actually means that they are staying focused on what is being said rather than being distracted with all the other stimuli that are being thrown at their brain pigeonholes. In fact, some studies have suggested that autistic individuals may actually have enhanced attention to verbal information as some have shown themselves able to process spoken language more efficiently when not having to make eye contact[21]. This suggests that nonverbal cues, such as eye contact, may not be as essential for communication as previously believed. For some autistic individuals, it can be a very intimate act to share eye contact

– one they feel more comfortable reserving for those with whom they are most familiar with. Other autistic individuals may go as far as using other communication methods (such as sign language or written communication) to avoid the discomfort associated with eye contact[22]. Meanwhile, others will learn to perfect eye contact as part of their masking, but they will drop that mask at some point and either stare without blinking or blink too frequently as the whole act is staged by masking. In some cultures, eye contact is also reserved for certain situations, but in our neurotypical world, when an autistic person is not perfect at maintaining eye contact, it can be misconstrued as their being either dishonest or not interested in the conversation.

"I was so excited as this was my first romantic date in university! But after a few minutes, my date looked at me and said, 'You are creeping me out.' Not what I wanted to hear on a first date! So, I asked, 'Why?' to which he responded that I was staring at him, so I asked what he preferred. He shrugged his shoulders and said that other girls, or his friends, usually blinked every three seconds or so. Since then, I religiously learnt to blink every three or four seconds when making eye contact. While the date didn't work out, as I could barely remember his name while having to secretly

> *keep counting and blinking every four seconds, it taught me one of my best masking strategies, which I still use to this day. I didn't know I was autistic at that time, but what a lesson to learn – and I still use it, even if it means I barely catch what I am being told!"*

Annoyingly Over-Questioning

This particular issue tends to really rile people and is another one of the "unspoken rules" that often create difficulties for many autistic individuals. There appears to be a secret and rigid limit to the number of questions one can ask before it becomes perceived as rude, intrusive, annoying or inappropriate – and autistic people never got the heads-up about it or received guidance on how to recognise when approaching that limit. Autistic people ask questions because they genuinely do not understand something, just like anyone else would. You might not understand why they are asking these questions, but trust us, it is not to vex you! Neither are autistic people in the habit of entering into pointless social interactions just for the sake of it. You might think they are asking basic or silly questions, with seemingly obvious answers – but clearly, they don't know the answer or else they would not be asking!

Autistic individuals may ask a significant number of questions, which can sometimes frustrate the neurotypical individuals in the interaction. This frustration might lead them to assume that the person on the spectrum is being sarcastic or mischievous, resulting in passive-aggressive behaviour such as ignoring or excluding the autistic person or even snapping at them. Again, just to reassure our neurotypical fellows who are reading this book, autistic people do not do this with the intention of annoying you, mocking you or wasting your time. They simply seek clarity. Unless you explicitly specify, "We have X amount of time to talk" or "Please limit your questions to three", they will not be aware that there is an unspoken limit to the number of questions they can ask. Autistic people struggle with unspoken expectations, and some do not grasp these social norms unless they are communicated clearly or learned by rote, similar to how one learns algebra. Furthermore, it is also important to note that not all autistic individuals will ask many questions during conversations. Individual communication styles may vary[23], or the autistic person might have had negative experiences that have taught them to suppress all their questions, including important or insightful ones. As a matter of fact, if an autistic person is asking a lot of questions, that is a sign that they are genuinely interested in the discussion and will probably have unique input to offer. If you nurture their participation by welcoming it and encouraging respect and patience, you may discover innovative and valuable contributions from them.

Fault Finding and Jumping Between Subjects

Similarly, some autistic individuals may be perceived as nit-picking during conversations as they often focus on details and have a strong need for accuracy. Neurotypical readers, PLEASE do not take this as a personal vendetta against you or as an effort to sabotage or belittle you – the person is simply trying to understand all the details that are known so they will be in the best position possible to ensure a positive or perfected outcome.

Moreover, though autistic individuals may seem to change subject at random, this is due, again, to their detail orientation and tendency to make links between seemingly unrelated subjects because of their focus on detail. Often, when AS people are perceived as attempting to avoid difficult conversations or manipulate a situation, they are actually trying to find more details or potential connections on a subject to which they are paying close attention. However, if they repeatedly divert the conversation, it is worth asking them about it directly, as this may be an indication that they are finding it challenging to cope with the situation and require some time to think, process it or be alone.

Detail Flooding

Another aspect influenced by this attention to detail is that most autistic individuals operate on a level of detail that most neurotypical people are not aware of. When asked a question, an autistic person may provide an exhaustive and honest answer rather than a brief and concise answer; this is because they want to ensure that they provide all the information needed for the other person to fully understand the topic or be enabled to make an informed decision. Since they may not know what specific information is needed, or what response the person asking is hoping to elicit from them, they may want to make sure that they are not omitting any potentially helpful details – hence the overwhelming amount of information in their response. This behaviour is not meant to be overwhelming or evasive but to be helpful and transparent. So, if you want specific information from an individual on the spectrum, the best approach is to directly ask them for it and be specific. They will appreciate your directness and gladly provide you with the information you seek.

> "My interviewing colleague asked the candidate to tell us about themselves. The candidate went on way too long, getting into their childhood dreams, which family members were still alive versus who had passed away, etc., and it was a bit awkward to stop them. However, had we been clearer from the start by saying, 'Tell us about your career and academic background in less than two minutes,' the candidate would have stuck to that, precisely."

Brief Answers

As confusing and as contrasting as it may be for the neurotypical person, autistic people may sometimes respond with a single word or a direct answer to a yes/no question without adding the social embellishments that neurotypicals expect. Though this might come across as rude or immature to neurotypicals, it is simply the AS person's direct way of answering the question that they heard, without any intention of causing harm or showing disrespect.

"My teacher asked if I wanted to have my breakfast. I responded, 'Yes'. She asked again, and I thought she didn't hear me, so I repeated my 'Yes', but a bit louder. She got angry with me and said I would have to wait until the following break to get my food when I knew how to answer better. By the time lunch break came, I was famished and dizzy; the moment she asked if I wanted my sandwich, I mustered the answer and said, 'Yes', to which she replied, 'What's the magic word?' I was too hungry and confused to think, so I quoted a magician in the book we were reading and said, 'Abracadabra?' The teacher told me to go back to the end of the queue and think about my behaviour. I must have passed out as I remember a nice teacher giving me a juice on the floor and then helping me to eat my sandwich while I was regaining awareness. She asked me why I was rude to the other teacher, and I didn't know why I was thought of as rude when I was the most well-behaved kid in the class and always followed instructions, cleaned up and helped tidy. So, I burst into tears and asked how was I rude, to which she replied, 'You kept saying "Abracadabra" when she was asking what was the magic word.' I asked the nice teacher, 'What IS the magic word if it's not abracadabra?'

and the look on her face made [it] clear that she realised how bewildered I was with unspoken pleasantries. She then taught me how to communicate with all the fluffy niceties...and boy, did I learn and get good at it! The next time the first teacher asked me if I wanted my sandwich, I responded by elegantly saying 'Why yes please, ma'am. I am overly excited to feel the bread as my teeth go through it and the crunchiness of the cucumbers inside – you see, ma'am, my mum doesn't like cucumbers in her sandwiches, but I do, as I find the coolness fascinating. What a nice teacher you are, storing our sandwiches in the fridge by name, and then distributing our sandwiches to us and not getting them mixed up, even if you have to take a small bite off some to ensure that they are safe for us to eat.' Guess what? Yes, that's right – I was punished for overtalking and mocking the teacher – the same one who had an issue with me responding too briefly! As an adult, I still get into trouble for both being too brief or being too detailed in my responses, when the person asking the question could make it easier on both of us by quantifying the response they are expecting."

Silence or Mutism

Yes, it is a spectrum after all! There can be many different reasons why autistic individuals may retreat into silence. Let's start with the most common one, which is that for many autistic individuals, the world is a VERY noisy place; in order to reduce overwhelm, it is natural for autistic people to try to cut out as much unnecessary noise as possible as their brains don't do that automatically.

> *"I asked my colleague what he could hear at that point, and he answered, 'You talking, and our colleague typing.' I explained that I could hear him talking, our colleague typing, our other colleagues outside the meeting room typing and talking, the traffic outside the window, and activity around the water cooler with the sound of electricity or the lights buzzing – and I heard all of it as loudly as I heard him. Only then did he realise why I have to shut down so many noises, and why I might not hear him if he doesn't tap my shoulder when talking to me – even if he said my name."*

Another reason why an autistic individual may go silent during a conversation could simply be to allow their brain the space to absorb and process what has been said to them. Or they might do it so they can analyse different scenarios in their head or relieve the strain of masking. However, it may also be because of what is known as situational or selective mutism, which is a temporary inability to speak or communicate during stressful or overwhelming situations. This can be caused by a variety of factors, including processing information or emotions, feeling overwhelmed by sensory stimuli or frustrating and unequal/unfair conversations, sudden changes of plan, or masking for too long. However, as we have discussed with other myths, while situational mutism may be more common in autistic individuals, neurotypicals are not immune to it, and those who have experienced it can appreciate how depleting it can be when trapped in social situations where communication is expected[24]. Being unable to communicate can lead to feelings of frustration and anxiety for both the individual and those who are communicating or living with them. It is important to recognise that situational mutism is neither a conscious choice nor a behaviour that can be controlled, and that telling an autistic individual to "use their words" or that they "can't just ignore the situation" can be extraordinarily destructive and dismissive. Instead, it is important to provide the AS person with support and understanding and to work with the individual to find alternative methods of communication, if necessary, or allow them the space to decompress.

"I don't understand why it is called selective mutism; I genuinely do not select it or want to go through it, and when it happens, it is like my soul has been shattered and scattered everywhere, and I am left subconsciously trying to gather and join the pieces back together so I can be human and feel again. Fortunately, my partner is very supportive – when it happens, he leaves me for a bit to recover or simply sits next to me quietly and holds my hand. I have had situations where I was devastated after having lost people that I love and was shouted at for not picking up my phone so I could receive someone's condolences or texting people back when I literally couldn't speak. That is very selfish and as inhumane as telling someone to stop crying when they've just lost a loved family member."

No Understanding of Hierarchy

Okay, so this one is *slightly* untrue, as autistic people do, in fact, understand nature's food chain and other logical hierarchies; if an autistic individual sees a lion, they will most likely run! However, autistic people tend to treat everyone equally, regardless of authority or established hierarchy, as they feel we are all still fellow humans regardless of our jobs or titles. Although some might appreciate the honesty of this direct approach, other senior or authority figures may punish or retaliate against the autistic person for not following the standard conventions surrounding hierarchy norms. It's like we mentioned before: autistic people are actually very good at following rules – just not unspoken rules.

> "...Haha, we are so good at following rules, we don't know what to do in situations where others DON'T follow the rules and lie or steal – or when someone behaves unethically at work, regardless of how senior the perpetrator is. I once saw the head of the department take something that was not his, and without hesitation, I said to him, 'That's not yours! Why are you stealing it?'"

Moral Superiority Issues

As demonstrated in the example above, consistency and justice are significant concepts for many autistic individuals (which is one reason why autistic people can be less prone to displays of unconscious bias). They often seek (and expect!) to find justice and fairness in their daily lives. This desire for consistency is not necessarily driven by a sense of moral superiority or naivety but rather by a deep need for predictability and stability. Autistic individuals may become vulnerable or confrontational when they perceive there to be inconsistencies or injustices in their environment. Therefore, it is important for those interacting with autistic individuals to strive for consistency in their actions and communications. After all, it's not so bad to aim to be consistent and not biased, is it? Is that not what all organisations should be aiming for?

> *"I saw how a colleague was treated compared to other colleagues. I tried to speak to the right people to get him the correct support, but instead, I got in trouble for pointing out how unethically or incorrectly he was being treated. We are all human and united in one organisation, why do some get treated differently/negatively compared to others? Either we are harsh with all or favour all or are simply professional and objective with all."*

The Autistic Person Refuses to Recognise that Autism is a Disability

This is very common. Imagine living your whole life not knowing that you have a disability; you have always felt like the world was harsh and difficult to understand and that you were extremely misunderstood but did not have the words or understanding to express it or just assumed that was the case for everyone else too. The misunderstanding and lack of support mean that you may even start to self-isolate and reduce your social interactions as you become more hurt and number. Then, suddenly, one day you get told you have a condition called autism, which is a hidden disability with no treatment that is not easily accepted by society. The good news is that you now know that all the difficulties you have been facing have not just been you, but others have it too due to the unaccommodating, neurotypically-designed world you have been living in. The bad news is that you can only succeed by taking on the full burden of the responsibility and strain of continuing to fit into this neurotypically rigid world. It would be a lot to take in at once, wouldn't it? Well, because the individual was not aware of their disability until later in life, late diagnosis can also often result in the autistic person not realising that they face discrimination or ableism when they do. This lack of awareness may result in difficulties advocating for themselves or ending up in vulnerable situations because they don't recognise the ableism that's being directed towards them. This is one of the reasons why it is so important for individuals with autism to receive proper diagnosis and education about their condition in order to better understand and recognise ableism and to advocate for themselves and others. It is also why it is so important to have autistic, allistic (non-autistic) and neurotypical allies all working in concert for the betterment of all neurotypes.

Disclosing is Not Always the Best Option

Many individuals who have been diagnosed with autism are encouraged to disclose their condition – both at work and to their family and friends – so they can best receive support and accommodations. While some return to the autism service with positive feedback about how well their disclosure went, the majority report that their relationships with colleagues, friends and family members deteriorated after disclosing their autism diagnosis. Many report that even when they were not responsible for certain issues, they were still blamed for them. Despite being reassured that their needs would be taken into consideration and that they would still be employed at work, loved elsewhere, respected and included post-disclosure - many found that, from the moment they first revealed their authentic selves, they often faced negative consequences for it and were forced to retreat back into masking as a result. This is understandable; it can be a big change for those around them to see this version of their loved one that they have not seen before and accept that this is the same person they thought they knew. As for work, according to City & Guilds' most recent report[25], 72% of people do not share that they are neurodiverse due to being worried about the impact disclosing would have on their career and prospects.

Rejection Sensitivity Dysphoria (RSD)

While we are on the subject of negatively perceived things, we should also cover rejection sensitive dysphoria (RSD). RSD is a term coined by William Dodson to describe an intense emotional response to perceived rejection, criticism or failure. It is a common experience for individuals with ADHD, but recent research has suggested that RSD may also be a common experience for some individuals with autism[26]. Negative interactions, such as being ignored, overlooked or directly rejected, can trigger intense emotional reactions in individuals with RSD. This can be linked to the amount of criticism, anger and negative messages hammered into the neurodivergent child while they are growing up. These emotional reactions can range from feelings of sadness and worthlessness to intense anger, burnout or meltdown, long-term depression, and anxiety. It is important to note that not all individuals with autism experience RSD, and not all individuals with RSD experience burnouts or meltdowns. However, for those who do experience RSD and its associated burnouts or meltdowns, it is important to learn strategies for effectively managing emotions and avoiding triggers that can lead to negative interactions.

Different Cultures, Different Interpretations

"I get frequently labelled as 'rude' when I communicate directly. I worry about sharing my ideas for fear of upsetting people with my directness or how I may speak. Their neuro-interpretation of MY actions or communication is perplexing for me and leads me to question my experience of the world, and that in turn makes me question my own actions and motivations in navigating the world."

In her book *Watching the English*, Kate Fox[27] highlights how different cultures can view certain traits of autistic individuals in different ways. In one example, she discusses how earnestness (which can include a predilection for telling painful truths or giving "unnecessary" details in conversation), a common trait among many autistic individuals, is considered a flaw or negative trait in some cultures; we will not name names, but British cultures, we are looking in your direction! However, in other cultures, this same tendency towards earnestness may be valued and appreciated. As you may have noticed, we have talked extensively in this chapter about how some autistic traits may be interpreted as "strengths" in one context and "challenges" in another. It is worth keeping in mind that these interpretations can also vary greatly by culture, so autistic traits that would be received negatively in one country may receive a far warmer welcome in another.

To Finish Off…

The common association between autism and social communication deficits often overshadows any interaction with an autistic person, laying the full blame for any communication issues on the autistic person. This is known as the concept of "double empathy", and it is extensively discussed in studies, especially in the works of Damian Milton[28]; it sheds light on the difficulties autistic individuals may face when interacting with neurotypical individuals. Milton explains how these social difficulties have traditionally been viewed as a one-sided problem entirely caused by the autistic person's struggles to relate to neurotypicals rather than a two-sided problem arising from differences in communication or understanding on both sides. Simply put, the challenges that an autistic person faces when it comes to interacting socially stem as much from the neurotypical person's inability to communicate with them as it does from the autistic individual's struggle to relate to neurotypical people. Milton elaborates that while autistic individuals remain hyper-aware of these differences in communication, they work harder to overcompensate for them than the allistic and exercise an immense tolerance when communicating with neurotypical individuals to try to fit in. Neurotypical individuals, on the other hand, tend to make little to no effort to try to understand or take responsibility for accommodating the differences in communication with neurodivergent people.

> *"When my friend turned around and asked me, 'Do I look fat in this?' I looked, and indeed, the colour did not compliment her body shape; so, I innocently responded, 'Yes'. After hours of crying and jogging compulsively on the spot (as if that was going to have an immediate effect on her physique), I was taught that instead of saying, 'Yes', the correct answer would have been, 'Of course not...but you do have other dresses that look even better.'"*

In conclusion, understanding the unique challenges faced by autistic individuals is critical to fostering empathy and creating a more inclusive environment. As we discussed above, between having to navigate a world filled with overly bright lights and overwhelming sounds, straining to mask, being misunderstood at every turn, and all the other day-to-day work-related traumas they experience, it should come as no surprise that many people on the spectrum struggle with mental health issues, including depression and severe anxiety.

It is essential to recognise the importance of mutual understanding and improve communication between autistic and allistic individuals to help bridge the gap between the two and promote greater acceptance and inclusion. We can't believe we had to use a whole chapter to explain this and bust myths, but here we are!

> *"Trauma changes the brain, but so does healing. There are many organisations and leaders out there that are truly inclusive – and they are the ones who reap the benefits, and loyalty, of a healed autistic individual."*

> *"I did not even know I was on the spectrum then; but being as inclusive as he was and wanting his team to thrive, he sat us down (individually) and explained where our strengths were and where we would need to train or change approach to be able to get my promotion in 18 months. It was objective, respected my gender and other characteristics, easy to follow, direct and embraced with trust and confidence. He looked at our team based on potential and made sure each one of us was trusted with responsibilities that allowed us to demonstrate our skills, grow and shine."*

CHAPTER 5

Why Does It Matter?

Let's look at some numbers again....

1 in 50 people are diagnosed as autistic; some believe that the actual number is more like 1 in 25, given how many people on the spectrum still go undiagnosed. About 80% of diagnosed autistic individuals (and who knows how many more from among the undiagnosed population) are unemployed or underemployed. 61% of these un/underemployed people are desperate to work, and 51% of those 61% have no financial means or government benefits (a problem that is exacerbated by the fact that the application process remains very unapproachable and disabling for autistic people, regardless of what the government claims). These unemployed or underemployed

autistic people possess many abilities and positive traits that could benefit the workforce – some that we have already discussed, some that are not covered in this book – and many of them would have a strong affinity for STEM (science, technology, engineering, and mathematics) related roles.

On that note, according to a 2021 Institution of Engineering and Technology skill survey and report[29], it is estimated that there is a shortfall of 173,000 workers in the STEM sector in the UK alone, which is costing the economy over £1.5 billion per annum. The rate of new and skilled workers joining the industry is growing far too slowly on an annual basis to sufficiently address this shortfall. What a catastrophe for organisational, economic and national growth!

But, as it just so happens, several studies have found a strong correlation between autism and STEM careers – what a coincidence, right? Remember that 80% of the autistic population that is unemployed or underemployed and desperate for work?! It sounds like we have just found an untapped, and highly relevant, talent pool!

"While he couldn't do eye contact or present well to his colleagues, he was the fastest at scripting codes and never had to search or look up syntax. It was like he spoke Java better than he spoke English! We had two developer roles advertised at the time, but after he started, we realised that we did not need another developer as he covered both jobs. If anything, all we needed was someone to explain and bridge the coding for the non-technical team members or to do the tasks that hindered his performance but that others would either enjoy or not mind. Sometimes we had to remind him to go home as one time we all left the office and realised the next morning that he spent the whole night working; he had no other plans, so he just forgot to go home to change his clothes, eat or sleep. We gave him a week off as he did five days' worth of work overnight!"

One study[30] found that individuals with autism were over twice as likely (12%) to have a parent working in a STEM field (compared to 5% of neurotypicals), suggesting that there is a genetic component to the correlation. Another study[31] found that individuals with autism were significantly more likely to pursue STEM-related degrees than their neurotypical peers. An even more recent study[32] found that autistic adults were more likely to work in STEM occupations than non-autistic adults. The study uncovered that 33% of autistic adults worked in STEM occupations, compared to only 23% of non-autistic adults – and these startling figures are just for diagnosed autism. We are not even talking about other neurodiversities here, such as ADHD, dyslexia, or dyspraxia, amongst others. And in case you were wondering, the research also showed that autistic adults in STEM careers reported higher job satisfaction because they enjoyed being utilised effectively. These findings, along with others, suggest that autistic individuals have a unique set of skills and interests that are well-suited to STEM careers. However, it's important to note that not all autistic individuals will be interested (or excel) in STEM fields and there are many other factors that may influence their career choice.

Again, Why Does it Matter?

Until June 2022, autism was classified as a mental disorder in the UK. Only then was it realised that autism, in and of itself, is NOT a mental disorder, and that it is, in fact, over-masking, a lack of reasonable accommodations, social adversities, or a combination thereof that results in those on the spectrum suffering from mental health issues or disorders. Unlike other conditions, there is no pill that can be prescribed to reduce the adversities faced by the autistic person in a neurotypical world or reduce the traits that society frowns upon; their options come down to pure masking and their individual tolerance for overwhelming stimuli and aggressions or exclusions.

Unfortunately, most autism funding goes towards finding out why autistic people are autistic (genetic research, etc.); about a quarter goes into ways to make autistic people less autistic (e.g., masking or learning how to fit in better), and less than 10% of autism funding goes into services designed to directly assist or enable autistic people. And no, we don't consider funding for initiatives to make autistic people less autistic empowering – or all that "helpful", for that matter. If you are neurotypical, please understand that "acting less weird", "fitting in", or masking in general can be very detrimental for an autistic person. Try to imagine how tiring it would be if you had to carefully modify and police your own behaviour every second you spent around other people, always hiding your true self for the sake of "fitting in". Now imagine having to do that endlessly – day after day, week after week, year after year, forever – and still being misunderstood. That is what your autistic friends, family members and co-workers experience each and every day – and it is exactly why we cannot be inclusive without accepting other people's rights to neuro-expression and to be authentically autistic without constantly accommodating neurotypical expectations or harsh environments that flood their senses.

I understand that, as humans, we have been hard-wired to be scared of variety; so, we try to mould everyone into one big category that says they are "normal" or "average". Until this day, there are even camps that aim to make autistic or LGBTQ+ youths more "normal". Take a minute though to imagine what the world would be like if everyone became "normal". What does "normal" even mean? As Charles Addams once said:

> *"Normal is an illusion. What is normal for the spider is chaos for a fly."*

Imagine what it would be like once we all achieved that, and we all got complimented about how "normal" we were all the time.

So, I can hear you ask again: why does it matter?

Over 85% of autistic adults have some form of mental illness; most do not know it, and cannot even express it, due to the issues with alexithymia and interoception that we pointed out earlier. Autistic people in the UK are eight times more likely than the general population to die by suicide. The average life expectancy in the UK is 80 years, but the average life expectancy of a level 1 autistic person – which, just as a reminder, is still referred to as "high functioning" – is 55 years. For others on the spectrum, the average life expectancy is 39 years[33]. I think for the commitment, creativity, hard work and other perks that come with autism, or just as humans, we deserve better! Both employers and society at large need to understand that those on the spectrum are not unfeeling/emotionless, failed neurotypical people; they are perfectly good neurodivergent people who have been failed by a world designed for neurotypicals without the inclusion of people with other cognitive diversities in mind.

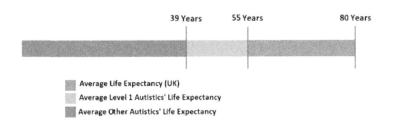

Figure 4: Average life expectancy

CHAPTER 6

What Do Organisations Do Wrong?

Everybody wants to be inclusive, and it is great to see the enthusiasm as organisations rush to be inclusive; but, all too often, inclusion becomes narrowly defined and overly celebrated, leaving those who desperately need it not being served or even more alienated than before the inclusion initiatives.

"Believe me when I say that I understand how scary change can be! But we have to start somewhere as this current system is just not sustainable anymore. It used to be women that were targeted, then black people, then indigenous people and people of other races, then those who had a gender change or were attracted to the same gender. And while they all have their challenges still, neurodivergent

> *people continue to suffer silently – and it is even worse if they are female or from other minority group intersections. "*

Despite the high prevalence of autism, many organisations still struggle to create an inclusive environment for neurodivergent individuals. A lot of organisations want to be inclusive but simply have no knowledge or experience of how to do that appropriately for those with cognitive diversities. Inclusion has been spoken about, and efforts at inclusion made, for people of different genders, cultures, ethnicities and other diversities. However, this most recent diversity is a bit harder (especially where there is intersectionality with other minority groups) as it involves a group that is less likely to speak out – even if they know that they are being mistreated – until the damage is already done. It also requires shifting from the long-held medical model to a social model approach and involves a whole new, under-researched diversity area with many spectrums in it – and no specific mould to fit all of them! These layers of complexity, along with a lack of understanding or lived experience, mean that even when organisations have the best intentions at heart, their efforts are rarely successful.

But that's why we were inspired to write this book – because we wanted to change all that! And if you are reading this, then we know that's a goal that you share too. We have already busted some of the myths and misconceptions that surround autism and discussed actions that should hopefully help to clear out some of those fallacies and allow a more inclusive environment to be created. Now, we can focus on the workplace and corporate side.

The following are some of the more common corporate mistakes that many organisations fall into without realising it, i.e., the kind of well-intentioned errors that lead organisations to rave about how neuro-inclusive they are, only to later realise that most of their quitting staff are neurodivergent people who have been failed by the organisation mistaking white-washing and toxic positivity for actual inclusion.

1. **A lack of widespread training on neurodiversity:** Autistic and neurodivergent individuals are often subjected to heavily individualised treatment, punishment and gaslighting due to a lack of organisation-wide awareness and training on neurodiversity. Research by City & Guilds[34] revealed that, in the UK, over three-quarters of human resource staff have had no official training on the subject. And a worrying percentage does not even consider neurodiversity as a hidden disability or something to take into consideration when hiring or firing! This issue can lead to a toxic work environment, with neurodivergent individuals feeling undervalued, unsupported and outcast. Raising awareness through training and education can be an enormous help in addressing this and other issues that may arise due to vulnerabilities or the desire to not stick out:

> *"I had a senior partner try to force himself on me; I assertively said that I was not interested and reminded him that he was a married man. A few months later, there were issues raised by the partner, and I mentioned everything that happened to an ally. They pointed out that what happened*

was wrong, and that I should not only respond to what was raised but report what had happened to HR. When I told the HR partner, he started off by gaslighting me, trying to convince me that the incident hadn't happened, until I mentioned there must be CCTV for that date and time, and he should obtain it. Then, not only did he ask why I didn't mention the incident sooner as it now 'sounded serious' (he didn't know that I had chosen to peacefully ignore it and try to move on as I did not want to make waves or get more attention) but he tried to coerce me into raising a grievance. I asked if this had happened before and I was told yes, that a female colleague had raised a similar grievance a year earlier against another partner. When I asked what happened after the grievance, I was told that the partner she raised it against committed suicide, leaving a wife and two kids behind, but that the colleague had kept her job. As if I would want to raise a grievance after hearing that! So, I resigned! When asked why I left that job (as it's always the candidate that's promiscuous with jobs and never management that's the issue /sarcasm), I simply said that the politics were not right for me after my two amazing managers quit. They would have understood and stopped a lot from happening, instead of gaslighting me on such a sensitive topic – they would have also understood that I came from a culture that would not be confrontational about such matters."

One of the most common mistakes organisations make once they have perfected the whole awareness-raising aspect is deciding to pat themselves on the back and leave it at that! While raising awareness is an important initial step, it is not enough in and of itself to create a truly inclusive environment. Organisations need to take concrete actions to accommodate neurodivergent individuals and ensure that they are fully integrated into the workplace. And no, this doesn't mean…

2. **Overreliance on individual accommodations:** While specific adjustments for autistic individuals may be necessary, they should not be a company's only focus; an organisation that plans accommodations strictly on an individual-by-individual basis is like a doctor who treats a patient's symptoms (for example, a cough) while ignoring the underlying condition (tuberculosis). Structural or systematic changes may be required to create a truly inclusive environment that meets the needs of all workers and ensures that neurodivergent individuals can also thrive within the workplace. This may include changes to an organisation's recruitment

processes, workplace culture and management practices.

3. **Throwing the burden on the autistic individual:** Accommodation processes should not place an undue burden on the autistic individual – that would defeat the entire purpose of working to accommodate them! It is important to strike a balance between accommodating autistic individuals' needs and not taking them away from their roles, sabotaging their efforts, hindering their career progression or causing them to spend more time on boring work. Organisations need to ensure that the accommodations they offer are designed in a way that does not add extra strain to the autistic individual's workload; if they do, that is neither equity nor equality. Managers play a crucial role in creating an inclusive workplace and need to be trained on how to communicate effectively with autistic employees and how to help make things better if their staff are not performing as expected. Shouting, targeting, creating punishment gaps, or putting employees on performance reviews without

first trying to understand their unique challenges and needs will only make matters worse. Managers who engage in those behaviours, or any combination thereof, may lead to employees with hidden disabilities who feel failed by the organisation's non-inclusive environment quitting en masse. If they do, the organisation will end up with either a very homogenous workforce or one in which submissive and fearful neurodivergent and diverse individuals are crippled by low morale.

"They could have changed my role title to 'Slide Coordinator' as I was making slides for as long as I remember in that role and not really doing what I actually specialise in. When I raised my concerns, I was given more slides work in response (I wasn't even putting my own work into slides but coordinating other people's input and putting that into slides) and told that I need to sell myself and find my own opportunities – the two exact things that I struggle to do! I was given no training, there was no equity and, unfortunately, there was no equality either as when I did do amazing slides, and projects were done amazingly, I was still scrutinised over small mistakes and the credit for those successes went to others."

4. **Viewing autistic traits as a performance issue:**
    Neurodivergent individuals are often subjected to
    negative performance reviews and denied leadership
    roles due to their autistic traits, which can include
    difficulties with social interaction, communication and
    providing "too much detail" (since, as we have
    discussed, people on the spectrum seem to have missed
    the hidden memo on how much detail is too much).
    This attitude can be harmful and lead to further
    discrimination against autistic individuals. Instead,
    organisations need to embrace and value the unique
    strengths and perspectives that neurodivergent
    individuals can bring to the workplace. Autistic traits
    can also offer unique strengths and skills that should be
    valued and celebrated – especially since they also
    happen to be protected disability characteristics (if you
    want to get legal about it and tick some diversity
    boxes). Training for managers to learn how to ask if
    autistic employees are doing alright and how
    management can help make things better if they are not
    can work wonders. As we discussed, shouting,
    targeting or putting your autistic staff on performance

reviews will only make matters worse and show that you are neither inclusive nor welcoming all to the table. An open, positive and helpful attitude when it comes to handling performance with neurodivergent staff can go a long way – but you need to be open to serving and leading your team to success.

5. **Exclusion from diversity and inclusion programmes:** Many workplaces have diversity and inclusion programmes that fail to mention autism or neurodiversity in general. This oversight not only reduces the efforts to raise awareness of neurodiversity issues or their existence but also fails to recognise the intersectionality of neurodivergent individuals with other diversities.

In conclusion, organisations need to do more than just raise awareness of autism and neurodiversity; they need to take concrete actions to accommodate neurodivergent individuals and create an inclusive workplace that values their unique strengths and perspectives. Organisations also need to reflect and measure their results to ensure that they are truly serving those they are trying to include and that their efforts are working. Those that do can reap the benefits of a truly diverse and inclusive workforce.

The Cost of Being Neurotypically Rigid

> *"Ableism is yet to experience the large-scale awareness raising and fightback that sexism, racism and homophobia have experienced, and continue to experience, but not at the scale they did 50 or 100 years ago."*

All the struggles that we have mentioned above, along with other societal expectations, treatments and experiences, can lead to what is known as autistic trauma. While some of these experiences may sound simple, non-intentional or mild to neurotypicals, they can lead to mental health conditions (such as autistic burnout, depression, anxiety or even complex PTSD (post-traumatic stress disorder)) that are amplified for the autistic individual, causing even more trauma. Unfortunately, trauma is very common with autism, and the trauma that is experienced by autistic individuals is often compounded by neurotypical society's tendency to overlook or ignore the impact of its actions on people on the spectrum. These traumas also tend to exacerbate autism's non-positive traits, making it more challenging for AS individuals to cope and increasing the strain of masking. Some common actions that autistic individuals see at work, and in society as a whole, that may contribute to autistic trauma may include:

- Social malice: This can take the form of microaggressions or being ignored, both of which can make autistic individuals feel unwelcome and misunderstood. They may also experience something known as perceived social ineptitude, where their difficulty engaging in social situations is interpreted as incompetence, a lack of effort or laziness.

- Being forced to mask or hide autistic traits: This includes being told that these traits are deficits that need to be stopped and invalidation of the autistic individual's needs. This can cause significant emotional distress and lead to a loss of identity and self-esteem.

- Communication invalidation: This occurs when the autistic person is interrupted or not listened to when they are trying to communicate; this may lead to the autistic person feeling misunderstood, frustrated, ignored or worthless. In addition, autistic experience invalidation occurs when individuals are told that their autism is not a "real" condition, or that they are just "quirky", or that their autism should not be used as an excuse for being lazy, slow or <insert negative adjective here>!

- Bullying or labelling can also lead to social exclusion, causing harm to an individual's self-esteem and emotional well-being.

- Interactions with neurotypical individuals: Even something as simple as an unplanned or intense interaction with a neurotypical colleague who is especially angry, excited or ecstatic can trigger negative thoughts and long-term issues in a person on the spectrum. These interactions may cause autistic individuals to feel like they do not fit in or are not understood, leading to feelings of worthlessness, isolation and anxiety[35].

> *"Oh, and let's not forget that it's all too easy to dislike a colleague who might not smile at you, or not know when to stop talking, or not greet you in the morning. We autistic people know that we are not always easy to like and rarely popular, but in the same way that we offer respect to others, and don't humiliate or shout at them, and give everyone a chance regardless of unconscious bias, we would hope that others can treat us with just a small part of the same dignity and objectivity we give out."*

- Being judged harshly: Being judged harshly due to miscommunication or misunderstandings is another form of microaggression that can have a significantly negative impact on autistic individuals and lead to feelings of inadequacy, uselessness and shame. This is amplified with those that have other intersectionalities.

- Being held accountable for role creep: This refers to employees being given new responsibilities without clear communication or the training that is required to enable them to succeed. Role creep can be especially hard and discriminatory for people on the spectrum.

- Not being allowed autonomy or trusted with decision-making: This is another microaggression that autistic individuals often face, which can result in them having to constantly validate or defend their actions, suggestions or decisions far beyond what their neurotypical colleagues are asked to. This has a direct impact on their confidence and self-esteem.

- In addition to microaggressions related to communication and decision-making, autistic individuals may also have their sensory hypersensitivity disregarded, challenged more harshly than a neurotypical colleague would or not accommodated at all – any one of which can lead to feelings of overwhelm, anxiety and distress.

"She was crying and rocking in the hospital bed, ignoring the teddy bear and the nurses who were trying to calm her down, until her mum arrived. The mother explained that they needed to dim the lights and lower the volume of the noises being made by the beeping monitors – and the moment they did, she began to calm down and gradually fell asleep. It wasn't the pain that had upset her, as they'd given her a painkiller, it was the aggressive sensory explosions that came with being in a hospital."

- Dehumanising processes or interventions: Including, but not limited to, seclusion or exclusion; these can result in traumatic experiences that can have a long-lasting, negative impact on an individual's mental health.

> *"I remember this kid in my school who told the teacher he couldn't participate in PE without his sunglasses as the sun was too intense for him. Instead of asking him more questions, the teacher told him that he had to go to detention and stare at the football field lights for the whole hour until he learnt to accept their brightness. Needless to say, that must have been tremendously harmful to him as we never saw him attend our school again. Many years later, we learnt that it was so overwhelming for him that he had a nervous breakdown from it, and unfortunately had to be home-schooled from then on due to the trauma of the sensory overload."*

It is essential to recognise the impact that microaggressions and other harmful actions have on autistic individuals (on everyone, really – but with autistic individuals, their effects can be more complex due to their vulnerability, an inability to stand up for themselves or realise what has happened later, and the deeper conundrums they experience) so that organisations can take steps to create more inclusive and supportive work environments. Providing accommodations and understanding the unique needs of autistic individuals are essential steps in preventing traumatic experiences for neurodiverse workers and improving the overall well-being of individuals with autism[36]. By doing so, we can create not just a diverse and inclusive workplace but also a world where everyone feels valued, included and empowered to bring out their authentic selves without fear.

> "It was very embarrassing having to listen to him shout, 'I don't understand what you are saying! I don't understand what you are saying!' over and over when I could clearly see by the reflection in his glasses that he was busy switching between different windows on his computer screen. I tried to explain it in three different ways, and he kept repeating that he didn't understand me. Doubting myself, I explained the idea to a colleague from another team, and he thought my explanation was brilliant the first time I went through it. I explained it to another colleague from my team, and they also agreed that my explanation was good from the first time and we needed to implement what I was proposing. I guess it was easier to say, 'I don't understand you' while being protected by his neurotypical privilege and seniority level rather than to admit, 'I was not paying attention' or 'This is what I don't understand.' I was scared of participating in meetings for months after that, to the point where I even started to stutter in conversations."

CHAPTER 7

Professionals on the Spectrum

Research has shown that, thanks to their unique strengths and perspectives, professionals on the autism spectrum have significant contributions to offer within their chosen fields. Some of our previous examples have highlighted how autistic individuals often possess remarkable attention to detail, exceptional skills in analytical thinking, unique insights and perspectives, and the ability to focus for extended periods of time. In addition, their affinity for pattern recognition and logical thinking can be highly valued in fields such as computer programming, engineering, and the sciences.

On the other hand, being on the spectrum can also present unique challenges for autistic individuals in the workplace. Some of the challenges that we highlighted include social communication and the interpretation of nonverbal cues, sensory sensitivities and a dependence on routines that can make it challenging to work in certain contexts or to adapt to changes in a fast-paced work environment. These challenges can lead to high levels of stress or burnout, depending on an individual's tolerances and masking ability.

As with all other aspects of the autistic experience, the impact that work has on the lives of autistic professionals can vary widely depending on an individual's specific challenges and strengths. For some autistic individuals, work can be a source of profound fulfilment and a way to express their interests and talents. For others, it can be an agonising struggle to keep up with the demands of a non-inclusive employer or unsympathetic neurotypical colleagues and to navigate the social aspects of their work environment as carefully as they would hidden landmines. The lack of adequate accommodations or support can make the workplace even more challenging or unbearable for autistic individuals:

> *"My best friend was a brilliant doctor – not the kind that does the bare minimum and tries to get rid of a patient the moment they were brought to A&E. She was fully dedicated, very thorough, ensured everything applicable was checked and always checked that the patient was assured and kept informed, chuckling or at least smiling. Thanks to the rigid, non-inclusive work environment and the unsupportive cultural environment around her outside work, she got to the point where she felt that she didn't belong; I was devastated when I learnt that she was no longer with us. This all took place in her late 20s after acing medical school. Another friend took his own life in his early 20s, as did another friend's loved school-aged niece and bright teenager [follow LinkedIn: #TheCaitlynConversation] – but the heartbreak doesn't end there as we continue to dismiss, gaslight and assume everyone fits into the same unbending neurotypical framework."*

Autistic individuals in the workplace must also contend with the stereotypes and misconceptions raised by media portrayals of people on the spectrum. As previously highlighted, media representations of autistic people often place an outsized focus on portrayals of individuals with savant syndrome. This has led to the creation of the "superhero narrative" – an expectation that ALL autistic people in the workplace will be savants with an array of veritable "superpowers" at their disposal. This can be harmful in several ways. For one thing, promoting the narrative that all people on the spectrum have "special powers" also sets the expectation that any autistic individuals who DON'T have unique abilities are somehow inferior or "less than"; in effect, it forces all autistic individuals without savant syndrome to feel like they must constantly justify their worthiness, or right to exist, without the "superpowers" that neurotypicals often believe come hand in hand with autism. And considering that only an estimated 10% of people on the spectrum display traits of savant syndrome[37], this means that the vast majority of autistic individuals who don't have savant syndrome must deal with this misconception at some point in their lives. The imbalance between expectations and the resources a person has; based on the above or the spiky profile is also a catalyst for autistic burnout.

The "superhero narrative" can also be seen in other aspects of the neurodivergent experience. One of the most troubling is the gender disparity in how it is often applied. Profiles of highly successful men who happen to be neurodivergent tend to link those two traits together, suggesting that their financial or creative success was achieved as a direct result of their neurodivergence. Successful businessmen like Richard Branson or Elon Musk, to name just two examples, often have their neurodivergence hailed as the source of their "eccentric genius". Highly successful neurodivergent women, on the other hand, are far less likely to have their neurodivergence characterised with the same degree of positivity or praise. Women are less likely to be diagnosed with autism at all, as they face more social barriers to diagnosis, and diagnosis – if it comes at all – is more likely to come later in life. When positive media portrayals of neurodivergence focus overwhelmingly on the experiences of privileged white males, it makes it all the more difficult for the many autistic individuals who do not fit neatly into that demographic to be accepted for who they are, rather than questioned, ignored or dismissed for who they are not.

A survey conducted in 2023 by Birkbeck's Research Centre for Neurodiversity at Work[38] and commissioned by Neurodiversity in Business found that two-thirds (65%) of neurodivergent employees in the UK fear discrimination from management, while more than half (55%) fear discrimination from colleagues. The survey also revealed that over 65% of managers said they did not have enough knowledge to support neurodivergent workers, and 30% of employers admitted to having "little faith" in workplace adjustments for neurodiverse employees. The survey also confirmed what we have previously discussed: hyperfocus (80%), creativity (78%) and innovative thinking (75%) were listed as being among the most positive aspects of neurodivergence, as identified by employers and employees alike.

It is important for workplaces to recognise the unique needs of autistic professionals and to provide them with accommodations and support as needed. Workplace accommodations, such as providing a quiet workspace, offering flexible scheduling or allowing neurodivergent employees to communicate via email or text, can make a significant difference for autistic individuals. This not only assists autistic professionals to overcome the unique challenges they face but also allows them to thrive in their chosen professions, benefiting others in their team in turn. Furthermore, fostering a culture of inclusion in the workplace can make a big difference to the experience of autistic professionals. This means creating an environment where individuals are respected and valued for their unique strengths, where differences are celebrated and where support is provided to help everyone reach their full potential. This type of culture can benefit not only autistic individuals but allistic employees as well, creating a more diverse and inclusive workplace that is better equipped to meet the needs of all. A rising tide lifts all boats, so if autistic professionals are provided with the environment and support that they need to flourish, then everyone – other neurodivergent employees (including undiagnosed ones), neurotypical employees, and managers alike – will reap the resulting benefits.

CHAPTER 8

The Neuro-Inclusive Workplace

> *"Change mostly happens due to challenges or breakdowns and rarely due to proactive forward thinking."*

In this chapter, we will look at how we can foster and enable an inclusive culture by considering the employee's work journey and identifying what a spectrum-inclusive workplace might look like.

We feel that it is important to emphasise that the concept of neurodiversity (or any diversity) within the workplace should not be reduced to a superficial exercise in meeting minimum legal requirements, an attempt to exploit the perceived strengths of neurodivergent employees, a catalyst to attract new talent or a market differentiator. While some neurodivergent individuals may have exceptional talents, work traits or savant syndrome, others may struggle with various challenges that impact their performance at work. It is not fair to expect all neurodivergent employees to possess extraordinary skills or to have to work harder than their neurotypical colleagues in order to earn a decent living. Neurodivergent people deserve to have an independent life and to make a living without the hindrances of unemployment or underemployment and without having to endure silent bullying or stressful work relationships that erode their self-esteem, dignity and mental well-being. These expectations are built on unaccommodating inclusions that are the outcome of neurodiversity being "sold" to organisations.

Organisations should prioritise the creation of an inclusive and supportive work environment that accommodates the unique needs of neurodivergent individuals. This means moving beyond tokenistic inclusivity to create a workplace culture that genuinely values neurodiversity and fosters mutual respect and understanding between neurodivergent and neurotypical employees. Accommodations such as flexible work schedules, clear communication and sensory-friendly workspaces can make a significant difference in enabling neurodivergent individuals to thrive in the workplace. The focus should be on providing a supportive and empowering work environment that enables all, including neurodivergent individuals, to live up to their full potential, while also recognising that neurodivergent individuals still deserve to have fulfilling and independent lives outside of work as well.

> *"Working in international firms, we do not tell our colleagues to change their accent when speaking to us; so, why is it okay to tell an autistic person or dyspraxic person to change how they speak or to mock their style of speaking, when others have no issue with it and can still understand the person. It is okay to ask them to slow down, repeat what they have said, or lower their voice for you – but it is not okay to label them as talking too fast/too slow or 'speaking weird' in front of a room full of people."*

As we highlighted in Chapter 5, less than 20% of autistic people are engaged in full-time employment in the UK, and 45% of the autistic people who have been hired have either lost or left their job due to miscommunications or being misunderstood. Here's one infuriating example:

> "I was disciplined for being abrasive/too direct with colleagues. Less than two months later, I was disciplined for being too detailed and not direct enough with colleagues. Others do not get told how unprofessional they are, even when shouting, but in my case, there was always room for discipline and 'your condition' being mentioned, even though they never mentioned my condition or disciplined me before I was diagnosed. Oh, and I was also denied promotions repeatedly for being too elaborate and 'rough on the edges' or 'too emotional' (yet somehow also disciplined for 'lacking emotion and networking'."

We have already explained how damaging masking can be as well as the human toll of workplace discrimination, which is truly heart-breaking and can lead to:

- Increased stress, feelings of isolation, anxiety and depression which can cause further mental health struggles.
- Not belonging or fitting in.
- Job loss and longer-term unemployment.

- Loss of income, livelihood and homelessness.

- Severe autistic burnout.

- Sense of worthlessness and depression.

Neurodivergent people are often singled out and harassed under the guise of performance management and face a disproportionate risk of losing their jobs and livelihoods because their brains work differently. Before entering a grievance or individual performance discussions or termination, there are points that the manager or leader should explore as we previously discussed.

"I was told that they were not able to find projects for me and that it was my duty to sell myself. Initially, while asking questions at the interview, I mentioned that I struggled to cold-sell myself unless I was selling a capability or extension of an existing project. In addition, my role was a technical role and not a sales role. This would be the case for those from humble cultures or certain females or those on the spectrum or maybe introverts. I asked if I could do sales training but was told that I didn't need training and I should continue to keep knocking the same doors, somehow expecting a different result from the same actions. None of my colleagues had to endure that lack of workplace psychological safety, turmoil and threat to their livelihood for months and more."

This should not come as much of a surprise, as a survey by City & Guilds and Do-IT Solutions[39] found that 77% of HR professionals and 71% of senior leaders have not had neurodiversity-specific training even within the past year. It is not all doom and gloom though; some steps have been made, as the survey also indicated that 41% of employers have adapted their recruitment processes to accommodate neurodivergent traits (though we will give these employers credit for having good intentions, we will discuss later why that is not the right step to start with). Further, almost half of the organisations that responded indicated that they did have neurodiversity champions or mentors on staff – but again, this puts the strain on the individuals and not on the system or processes that affect the organisation as a whole. Meanwhile, another survey conducted by Resource Solutions revealed that only 16% of UK workers felt that their employer is "very" inclusive to neurodivergent individuals; that number dropped to a measly 11% when the 25-34 age group was asked if their employers created an inclusive workplace. These statements alone shed immense light on why neurodiversity is a more challenging and feared diversity for organisations to deal with than most others, and to be fair to all the well-meaning workplaces out there…we get it! Take all the issues that we have discussed, add in the challenges that always come with making changes or facing the unknown, add in the lack of disclosure by neurodivergent employees fearful of retaliation and the trust that would need to be built to combat it, and it seems pretty clear why this can all seem utterly overwhelming for even the most experienced HR personnel and best-intentioned leadership. Oh, and of course, we also need to consider the fact that autism is both hidden and the most recent diversity being acknowledged. We get why the combination of all these challenges might encourage leadership to take shortcuts or to ignore the matter and hope that a few minimal changes will make the problem go away. After all, history has shown that the neurodivergent community will generally cause less of a fuss when things go wrong and are more likely to quit and deal with their mental health on their own.

Nevertheless, if we treat inclusivity for autism and neurodiversity as more than just a mere box-ticking exercise at work, then many of the above issues can be avoided, and we can all enjoy a much more inclusive, diverse and productive workforce. Inclusion statements alone will not do much other than promote an organisation at a superficial level while its non-inclusive environment damages more autistic and neurodivergent individuals. Concrete steps – including strong policies, training, and equality and equity initiatives – are what is actually needed for that untapped workforce to flourish and for organisations to reap the benefits as a result.

> *"I remember how I had an amazing manager who realised that there was an issue that caused my first salary to not get paid. The system didn't process me as an employee as I did not select my gender, which was 'optional'. Instead of forcing me to disclose my gender, he simply changed his record from 'male' to 'undisclosed', and that meant that he was not paid the following month. HR approached him and tried to fix the system promptly to accept 'undisclosed' gender entries. He did this to prove to HR that the system in place did not work, which triggered them to apply the inclusive change. Another manager would have forced their employee to mould or fit themselves into the faulty system."*

Setting up the right environment is key for success; think of exotic fish – they can serve as a brilliant, decorative and relaxing addition that looks amazing...but only in the

THE NEURO-INCLUSIVE WORKPLACE

right environment. You cannot bring tropical fish into a cold, chlorinated water tank and expect them to survive, let alone thrive. As many have pointed out – most recently Professor Nancy Doyle from Genius Within[40] – an inclusive workplace should not be a reactive place where people must be driven to their wits' end before putting their hand up and saying, "I need help, please." The onus for change should not be placed on the individual. We need to look at what people have asked for, change things based on the accommodations that have proven most successful in actual workplaces, both with people with lived autism experience AND also allistics, and then make that the standard going forward. We also need to be creative about it; if you want your neurodivergent staff to bring their full, creative selves to work, then you as leadership should be more creative at accommodating and supporting your staff so everyone is empowered to be their best, authentic selves.

> *"The systems were so rigidly in place, but they were not working. Neurotypical and neurodivergent staff alike were infantilised by the rigid systems and processes – but the neurotypical colleagues either quit and moved on or hid their struggle until they could move on."*

Simply put, leaders want engaged employees who can be efficient, innovative and contribute to a growing and thriving culture – and a truly inclusive environment that supports a broad spectrum of people and perspectives can deliver that competitive edge. Below are some practical tips that will aid you in making your workplace more neurodivergent-inclusive.

Change the Narrative and Context

Changing the narrative and context of autism within the workplace is an important step towards creating a more inclusive and supportive work environment for individuals on the autism spectrum. One way to change the narrative is to move away from the traditional deficit-based model, which focuses on the challenges and limitations of individuals with autism, towards a strengths-based model, which recognises and values the unique skills and abilities that individuals with autism bring to the table. By recognising and valuing these strengths, workplaces can create a more inclusive and supportive environment for individuals with autism and their other diverse staff (yes, this does include neurotypicals, who will still be cognitively, culturally or gender diverse).

Changing the context of autism in the workplace also involves creating a widespread culture of understanding and acceptance. We hope that the explanations, lived experiences and myth-busting sections of this book have opened your eyes and allowed you to gain a better understanding of your neurodivergent colleagues. If you recall the "double empathy" problem, then you will understand how important it is for neurotypical people to help shoulder their fair share of the load for reducing miscommunications with their neurodiverse colleagues. Steps to address this may include providing lived experience training and education to co-workers and managers on autism and how it may impact individuals in the workplace. Additionally, workplaces can look proactively to provide accommodations and support to individuals with autism, such as flexible scheduling or a quiet workspace, to help mitigate some of the challenges they may face.

CHAPTER 9

Employee Journey Solutions Dive

Research shows that many of the workplace adjustments that autistic people would benefit from most would also be beneficial to others, especially in culturally diverse organisations. For example, providing clear and direct communication does not only help autistic individuals but also employees who speak English as a second language or those who have difficulty with indirect communication styles based on their culture. Additionally, creating a quiet workspace or allowing flexible scheduling can assist employees who struggle with distractions or have family responsibilities as much as they would help employees on the spectrum. By implementing accommodations for autistic individuals, workplaces can create a more inclusive and supportive environment for all employees, resulting in increased job satisfaction, productivity and employee retention rates[41]. By implementing these practical solutions and encouraging a culture of inclusivity, organisations can create a more diverse and supportive work environment for all employees. Rising tides…remember?

You are probably thinking that we will start with hiring as that is the first part of the employee journey…but remember the exotic fish analogy? If we bring home the fish before setting up its environment, that will surely result in its untimely demise! Instead, we need to set up the right environment for it first – only then can we safely introduce the fish into it. There is a high chance that you already have some "exotic fish" in your organisation that can assist you in testing and perfecting your environment; in other words, before looking to hire new autistic or neurodivergent people, make sure you have created a good environment for those neurodiverse people who are already in your organisation. Hence, we will start the employee journey the other way around with inclusive hiring being the last element to look at. Setting up the right environment is key for success, so we will talk about inclusive hiring later.

Don't worry, we are here to assist and walk you through all of this!

Post-Hire

Inclusion is a choice that we make in every interaction and conversation, and it is particularly important to consider in the workplace when working with neurodivergent or other diverse individuals.

> *"In every interaction and conversation, we have the choice to be inclusive or exclusive."*

Creating an autism-inclusive work environment requires a multi-faceted approach that incorporates a number of different practical solutions. Here are some additional thoughts to help expand upon the points we have already mentioned:

- Promote education: The first way to promote inclusion is by educating both oneself and others on neurodiversity. This can include seeking out training and information on neurodivergent conditions or simply asking individuals about their preferences or the challenges they face without putting the whole onus for change on them. The more educated we can all become, the easier it will be to avoid making assumptions and to tailor our communication and interactions to be more inclusive.

- Offer choices and flexibility: Allow for different work arrangements, such as flexible hours or remote work options, to accommodate the unique needs of autistic individuals. Encourage staff to communicate their preferences and find ways to incorporate their feedback into the work environment. Use people according to their strengths and provide them options for different training plans, as needed.

- Responsibility of disclosure: When a team member discloses their neurodivergence, be mindful and respectful as it takes a lot of courage to disclose. Neither the organisation nor the manager should try to avoid the issue by either trivialising it or delaying dealing with the disclosure. When an individual has made the decision to disclose, the organisation needs to put the relevant support, adjustments or training in place to enable that team member to perform to their best potential.

- Sensory-friendly environment: In addition to leaving window seats/office spaces for those who need them, consider using natural lighting or softer LED lights to minimise sensory distractions. Offer noise-cancelling equipment such as headphones or earplugs to reduce auditory input and provide low-stimulation areas for breaks if space allows.

- Improve wayfinding: Make it easier for autistic individuals to navigate the office space by using clear signage and distinct colours to identify different areas. Avoid clutter and ensure that furniture is placed in logical locations.

- Active listening: This can be another key element of inclusion. It is important to acknowledge and credit autistic workers' contributions, invite contributions from all and intervene positively if micro-inequities are observed. This helps to create a culture of inclusivity where everyone feels valued and respected.

- Respect differences: Some people might need more time than others to answer questions verbally. They can be accommodated by sending out a meeting agenda in advance; also, be sure not to catch them out with the excuse that "this is how such matters are discussed with the rest of the team".

Leadership needs to have real buy-in and take neurodiversity integration seriously rather than just treating it as a tick-box exercise; this also extends to HR and their commitment to be truly inclusive and not merely check boxes or catch people out. On a similar note, leadership should look to avoid punishments that may be rooted in unconscious biases, can be publicly seen by other team members or could have a detrimental career impact. Avoid the glass cliff or punishment gap effects. Do not put people on the spot or make them feel intimidated or marginalised. Would you punish someone of a different race or gender or who is neurotypical in the same way for the same action? If not, avoid creating a punishment gap for your neurodivergent minority. Of course, you should still hold all team members accountable for their behaviour and performance, regardless of their neurotype or other characteristics. Don't overlook or excuse problematic behaviour or biases from certain individuals or groups. Foster a culture of participation, collaboration and respect. Create a safe and supportive environment where everyone feels heard and valued, and where diverse perspectives are welcomed and appreciated.

Non-verbal communication is also crucial for creating an inclusive environment. It is important to distribute eye contact – don't chase or demand it if it is not freely given – and consciously use an inclusive tone and body language. If a person avoids eye contact, continue to look in their direction without intimidating them into making eye contact.

While masking is an option, it can be exhausting and detrimental to the mental health of neurodivergent individuals. Instead of requiring the autistic individual to mask and bear the brunt of all the accommodations, we should focus on creating an environment where everyone feels valued for their unique strengths and abilities, even if we have to create the roles or tasks to enable them to shine once in a while. And, of course, a safe place for people to raise concerns.

Ultimately, that's what creating an inclusive workplace environment is going to require the most: an organisation-wide commitment to celebrating strengths and empowering individuals to be themselves. So, recognise and challenge your assumptions, avoid jargon, stereotypes, reading between the lines and avoid alienating people based on their neurotype. Take the guesswork out of communication by keeping your communication clear and direct, without making assumptions! Communicating clearly and honestly is especially important when it comes to deadlines or tasks. Leave nothing to be inferred; if you need something done in a specific way, say so. If one project or task is a priority, then make that clear without being judgemental or patronising. Many people sometimes struggle to retain information that has been delivered verbally, so if something is important, make sure to send that information by email to ensure that it will be easily accessible and in writing.

Avoid using labels or assumptions about someone's behaviour or abilities based on their neurotype. Instead, provide clear and objective feedback that focuses on the behaviour, not on the person. For example, if someone is speaking fast, you can ask them to slow down for you, without making assumptions about their communication style or personality. Be open and look to connect authentically with your autistic employees – just remember that while all humans are social creatures who crave connection, socialising in a loud and busy bar might be stressful for autistic individuals due to sensory overload.

That does not mean that the person would not enjoy a one-on-one or small group interaction or a purposeful social activity. Be open-minded in seeking ways to connect with your team and be patient if your autistic colleagues take a bit of time to warm up – they might have learned to avoid contact or be cautious about connecting due to having been burnt socially before.

Lead by example and promote a culture of inclusivity and equity. As a leader, it's your responsibility to ensure that everyone in your team is being treated fairly and respectfully, regardless of their background, identity, likability or neurotype. So, take an active role in promoting a culture of inclusivity and equity. Recognise and appreciate everyone's strengths and contributions and provide opportunities for growth and development for all. Ensure that you have truly created a welcoming and accepting environment where acceptance, accommodations, equality and equity are in place so that everyone can thrive. Ensure that it is safe, easy, constructive and nurturing to have difficult conversations – and ensure that those conversations go both ways (yes, managers do, in fact, make mistakes too)! Leaders set the tone in any environment; if you make it clear through words and actions that you take inclusion and equity seriously, then others will do so as well. Some other efforts that can be made to support inclusivity include:

- Supporting autonomy: Respect the autonomy of autistic individuals by allowing them to have a say in the accommodations and support they receive. There's no substitute for lived experience, so empower them to communicate their needs and preferences without judgement. Hiring or consulting allistic people on matters of autism gives the impression that the organisation is not comfortable hearing feedback from those affected, and that alone is a strong sign of mistrust and exclusion. This also affects the quality of the advice itself as it will be a neurotypical consultant's advice on something they have never experienced themselves. It would be as counterproductive as learning how to drive a car from someone who has never driven a car!

- Creating clear guidelines: To ensure that training, promotions and pay decisions are made fairly, it's essential to have an explicit, written framework that outlines how these decisions are made. Make sure your team understands this framework, and if they have any questions or concerns, be sure to address them promptly. To make performance reviews more objective, remove names and consider using colour-coded ratings to indicate performance. Use more specific language to describe performance, rather than relying on vague statements such as "a good team player".

- Fostering fair development: Developing your team fairly means providing everyone with equal access to high-potential assignments and ensuring that performance reviews, promotions and pay increases are based on merit rather than personality or likeability. It's important to acknowledge that some individuals may need to prove themselves more than others and that underrepresented individuals are often unfairly penalised via the punishment gap that we discussed earlier. By creating an explicit framework, establishing clear rules and using objective criteria to evaluate performance, we can also create more equitable processes.

- Avoiding confusing performance with potential: It's important to distinguish between performance and potential and to avoid judging individuals based on their personality or people skills relative to the majority of their colleagues. Research has shown that homogenous groups are often given the benefit of the doubt within the workplace, while underrepresented staff must work harder to prove themselves. Be honest with yourself and your team about any potential biases, conscious or unconscious, and make a conscious effort to disrupt them. Don't stereotype underrepresented groups or require them to conform to certain personality traits.

- Interrupting and addressing bias: To disrupt bias, it's important to call out and interrupt microaggression behaviours such as "bropriating", "manterruption", stereotyping and "whipeating". Establish a formal policy to address any instances of bias and implement it consistently. Remember, bias is worse for underrepresented individuals, so it's crucial to approach it in the right manner. By taking action, we can stop bias in its tracks.

- Empowering your team: To promote equity, it's important to give your team the tools and frameworks they need to advocate for themselves. This includes teaching them how to self-promote and defend themselves during performance reviews. If team members aren't receiving feedback from those they've worked with, step in and ask for it on their behalf.

- Adopting a different mindset: When we do see bias or microaggressions, our reaction should not just be about "who" did it; as with any other kind of mistake, we should not place all the weight and blame on one person but keep focused on trying to determine "why" and "how" did it happen instead. That way, we can ensure that it is not a single person bearing the weight that the system or organisation allowed; our goal is to prevent that "why" and "how" from being repeated with others in the organisation or in other situations in the future.

- Encouraging leadership role modelling: Senior leaders should talk openly about neurodiversity, encourage others to do the same and lead by example by being inclusive, understanding and supportive of autistic employees.

- Treating neurodivergent leaders fairly: Organisations should ensure that neurodivergent colleagues are not marginalised or underrepresented in leadership due to small traits or differences from the expected mould of leadership

- Finally, be aware of the reasons why team members might leave and conduct exit interviews to assess how well your team is performing with regards to inclusivity.

Remember that inclusion and disrupting bias is an ongoing process, and it will not happen overnight. Nevertheless, by taking action today, we can begin to create a more equitable workplace for all. If you unintentionally push bias onto a team member, apologise and look for ways to ensure that it doesn't happen again. And if bias persists, take more assertive action to disrupt it!

In conclusion, promoting inclusion within the workplace requires intentional effort and a commitment to education, active listening, the avoidance of assumptions and stereotyping, the creation of a welcoming environment and the celebration of individual strengths. By doing so, we can create a more inclusive workplace culture that benefits all employees, both neurodivergent and neurotypical alike.

Now that we have achieved the goal of promoting an inclusive environment, let us look at the hiring process and how we can make it more equal and equitable!

The Hiring Process

> *"I am often praised for bringing the best talent to organisations; it was my awareness of unconscious bias that helped me achieve that. While most recruiters would ignore a long CV or favour those that fit a set of rigid, not role-related criteria, I looked at all CVs with an eye towards evaluating the person's potential, rather than just what they say they have done. For example, not everyone (especially females, or certain ethnicities or other diversities) is good at selling themselves; they might say 'we' instead of 'I'. But many of those people who might struggle at selling themselves will do a brilliant job when hired, and as recruiters, we need to give a chance to the five-page CVs and humble applicants instead of following strict criteria to cut corners – and then complaining about how the talent pool is lacking diversity!"*

In order to develop a more inclusive hiring process, organisations should think about, and try to implement, the following points – not just to attract more neurodivergent individuals but also to improve diversity in hiring across the board:

- Competitive salary? Then be transparent about it! If you know what you are looking for in a candidate in terms of their experience and skills, and you know the budget that you have available, then just be upfront about the pay range or actual salary figure for the role; negotiating a better salary should not fall onto the autistic candidate as some will not play this game, and those who do may not be very good at it! Pay secrecy and the common practice of offering salaries based on someone's previous wage mark create hugely inequitable wage gaps; organisations that are genuinely committed to inclusivity are probably going to want to avoid underpaying their neurodivergent candidates!

- Consciously aim for diversity: Anyone who's ever taken an archery lesson, or learned to shoot a basketball, can attest to this one universal truth – you hit what you aim at. So, if you are not consciously aiming to promote diversity, it's not going to "just happen" on its own – or by hiring diverse people and not going further than that! All too often, when thinking about "cultural-fit", organisations enable exclusions by choosing people that fit within their usual "norm" or expected culture. If you are aiming for inclusivity, then assess people based on their skills, ability and experience rather than on how they speak or if they sound monotonous (unless the role involves speaking or presenting, of course).

- Application process: Would the role or applicant benefit from an alternative application process? Some organisations accept video CVs where applicants cover their experiences or CV over a recording; other organisations offer the option of answering five or six questions over recording, and from that, they invite the top candidates to the next round.

- Embrace transparency and objectivity: Use specific and objective benchmarks to rate all applicants; compile a list of what your expectations are in terms of experience, qualifications, requirements, skills and the qualities needed to succeed in the role, then ensure that your team agrees with your compiled list and that all those involved in the interviewing process follow the list objectively. If any list items are ignored or flagged for an applicant, find out why and track similar situations to ensure fairness. Similarly, try to be as specific and objective as possible with the job description and any required questions on the application; avoid exclusive or elusive questions like, "How good are you with *XYZ*?" Instead, ask "How would you approach this task on *XYZ*." Many neurodivergent applicants may struggle with an open or opinion-based question relative to a question that is more straightforwardly factual.

- Requirement: Use plain language and assess if the job really requires all that is required. Does it genuinely require a psychometric test? These can be excluding for many people and are not generally required for most roles.

- Apprenticeships: Applicants can show their strength if they have no previous experience or if they struggle with the usual reading and writing aspects but can still do a good job as an apprentice. There have been life-changing apprenticeships for candidates without the typical academic background and candidates whose jobs do not require a degree that is usually not relevant to what they actually do in the job.

- Interview process: some adjustments can include having a quiet zone in the office for the interview or allowing it to happen virtually. It can also be helpful to send the interview questions in advance of the interview day, share clear directions (with photos if needed) of how to get to the office and explain who the interviewers will be. Other useful adjustments could be sharing the agenda, avoiding generic, hypothetical or abstract questions, and professionally thanking and telling the candidate when they have answered the question. The latter adjustment can be particularly helpful if you have not specified how long you expect the answer to be as the candidate may exceed your uncommunicated expectation (also remember that they might take your questions literally). Other things to be more understanding about are that eye contact might not be what you are used to (either prolonged or fleeting as previously discussed) and the candidate might benefit from or need their notes or written tips in order to answer questions under interview stress which can impact their working or short-term memory.

"When the interviewer asked me 'why would we hire you instead of the other candidates', I asked if I could have a look at all the CVs shortlisted for the role. In my mind, I

> *could not genuinely answer that question without knowing how I ranked compared to the other candidates. It turned out that they just wanted me to talk about my skills and experience that made me stand out or perfect for the role"*

- Measure your efforts: the best way to know if something is working isn't to guess but to actually measure its effects! One way of doing this is to send a short survey to candidates who do not get the role, either because they were rejected or because they voluntarily opted out of the process. Ask questions like:

  o Did you feel that you had an equal opportunity to succeed in the process and get the role?

  o Did the hiring process allow you to showcase your qualifications, skills and expertise effectively?

  o Did you experience or observe any issues of bias, discrimination or inequity in the hiring process? Please elaborate.

- Hire process feedback can be eye-opening when it comes to assessing how candidate-inclusive your hiring process is. You can also look at the data from the hiring pipeline numbers to pinpoint where the candidates are dropping. For example, if many candidates start the job application and do not submit it, that could mean that either the format or the questions required are not user-friendly.

Reflections

"I was asked, 'How can you be a good leader when you are autistic?' I explained that while the traditional image of a leader is a white male who is tall, extroverted and fits a specific corporate template, there is far more to leadership than that. Traits that are commonly associated with effective leadership (as found in various leadership literature and studies) include highly passionate, strong sense of justice, out-of-the-box thinking, clear and deliberate communication, and a systematic approach to problem-solving. Meanwhile, traits that are commonly associated with autism include highly passionate, strong sense of justice, out-of-the-box thinking, clear and deliberate communication, and a systematic approach to problem-solving. In other words, how could I make a good leader when I was autistic? Because we make GREAT leaders if that is what we are interested in."

It is important to acknowledge that the current representation of autism in mainstream media and research is largely dominated by white, cisgender, Western individuals, often from middle-class backgrounds. That leaves out all the valuable insights and experiences that could be shared by people from marginalised communities, including people of colour, LGBTQ+, and the non-speaking autistic community. They are, unfortunately, the least likely to be represented, the most likely to be affected by masking and, in some places, not welcomed even within their own cultures or communities. We must actively seek out and amplify these voices to gain a more comprehensive understanding of autism. This is especially true for underrepresented and other marginalised communities who may face additional discrimination and bias. By being compassionate and accepting of autistic individuals regardless of whether they are or aren't wearing their mask, we can create a more inclusive and supportive environment for everyone, regardless of their neurodiversity.

CHAPTER 10

Conclusion

Now, that you have made it to the end, we hope that the lived experiences, the research, the stories and the insights that we have shared with you throughout this book have helped to open your eyes to some of the challenges and struggles that many of those on the spectrum may face each and every day. Even more importantly, we hope that it has inspired you to become a force for change and encouraged you to confidently tap into this hidden (and loyal) talent pool as a better-equipped leader of growth.

For many neurodiverse people, moving from the very organised and structured environment they grew up with at school and at home to the more fluid, unstructured environment they encounter in the workplace – and all the hidden communication that comes along with it – can be a transition filled with uncertainties. Yes, it is true that neurodiverse people may face many challenges that their neurotypical colleagues may not. Many of them do wind up un or under employed relative to their skill sets and experience, and they are more vulnerable to being misunderstood, misused or unappreciated by poor management.

However, as we have discussed, this also means that autistic individuals represent an untapped gold mine of talent that organisations are not currently taking advantage of (or are trying to take advantage of but not fully succeeding because of their approach towards inclusivity). Most organisations are either not using their neurodiverse talent to the best of their abilities, actively driving neurodiverse staff members away due to poor policies, systems designed for neurotypical staff, and a lack of suitable adaptations, or both – and we want to change that!

Over the course of the book, we have discussed the challenges faced by people on the spectrum, and for good reason – frankly, there are a lot of them! For many, merely existing in the modern world brings with it a whole host of difficulties that most neurotypical people will rarely have to worry about. Between having to navigate social norms and sensory sensitivities, activities that neurotypical people might engage in without giving them a second thought – such as taking a simple trip to the grocery store or eating lunch in a noisy canteen – can feel like completing a gruelling obstacle course for us.

But we did not want this to be a book that was just about challenges and struggles (even we wouldn't want to read that!) To us, this is a book about inclusion, hope and positivity and the possibility for change that would positively impact many – not just the neurodiverse.

If you take away only one lesson after reading this book, we hope that it's this: when a workplace becomes more inclusive, EVERYONE benefits. And we mean everyone – the neurodiverse, the neurotypical, staff, management, EVERYONE – and can you guess what that means? Yes, that's right, a happier, more innovative, more efficient and more productive workforce.

We believe that many of the issues affecting neurodiverse people within the workplace stem, ultimately, from a lack of awareness, a lack of understanding and lazy efforts at inclusion which can also negatively impact diverse neurotypicals. We believe that when organisations fail to support and raise up their neurodiverse employees, that failure is rooted not in malice or indifference but in ignorance; most organisations would want to do better by their autistic employees if they only knew how.

That is why we wrote this book: to transform misunderstanding and ignorance into understanding, acceptance, and awareness and thus enable more organisations to tap this hidden talent pool. At the same time, we wanted to show them exactly how they can best support and uplift their neurodiverse staff so that we can all benefit from the results. We hope that it has helped to raise your awareness and understanding of the world as it is experienced by people on the spectrum and that you will choose to join us in building a better tomorrow for all people, regardless of their neurotype.

"When a flower doesn't bloom, you fix the environment in which it grows. Not the flower."
~ Alexander Den Heijer

BONUS CHAPTER

Unconscious Bias and Busting It

Research[42] has consistently shown that diverse teams outperform homogenous teams, show more commitment, have better problem-solving capacities, come up with more innovative solutions and benefit substantially from collective intelligence. Despite knowing this to be true, organisations still seem to struggle when it comes to identifying and eliminating bias, even when they devote generous budgets to training and consultancies designed to combat it.

Firstly, we need to accept that when it comes to bias, "eliminate", in and of itself, is simply not a viable target. Unconscious bias is deeply ingrained in our minds; it's part of our evolutionary survival instinct, and to eliminate that would involve A LOT of heavy, conscious work. Therefore, a better (and far more practical way) of handling bias is to focus on interrupting or disrupting it.

Secondly, when we use the terms "majority", "minority", or "others", please do not assume we are referring only to traditional categories such as genders or ethnicities as bias can exist in many forms beyond these categories. While someone might be considered a majority in one industry or company, they could be considered "underrepresented" in another – and this is where leaders, HR and recruitment staff need to ensure that the employee's journey and commitment to integration are inclusive for all. Bias can also exist outside these criteria; there is also bias based on appearance or halo effect bias, for example.

So, in this bonus chapter, we aim to shed light on different types of biases, how to identify them (especially if you are not affected by the bias) and how to interrupt or disrupt them to enable a more inclusive employee journey and workplace!

The B Word

First, let's reflect on what unconscious or conscious biases may look like. Some examples may include the following[43]:

1. Tightrope: Narrower acceptance of the behaviour of "others" compared to one's own group.

2. Favouritism: Trusting certain individuals with bigger or better opportunities.

3. Prove it again: Having to prove oneself more than homogenous group members have to.

4. Maternal (or paternal) wall: Certain groups (initiated with mothers in mind) having their commitment and competence questioned.

5. Tug of war: Divisions arising due to "others" within the same minority having different strategies for assimilating with the dominant group (or refusing to do so).

6. And the most commonly discussed types: Gender and racial bias, which can reflect stereotyping or affinity bias, confirmation bias and the horn effect.

Unfortunately, while these biases exist in many places, they can be further exacerbated in group cultures and work environments due to institutional barriers and subtle dynamics.

Now, even if we spent all day walking around with the above in mind, would that mean that we would be able to recognise bias and disrupt it? Not really, as we would still need to take a deeper dive into our own biases in order to combat them effectively – and, if we ourselves are not affected by a bias, it can be very hard to recognise or respond to.

While subtle dynamics (also known as micro-inequities) might seem trivial, they tend to pile up and have a cumulative effect, and they are the main reason why heterogeneous or minority employees leave their jobs, regardless of their seniority in the organisation. These biases get even more accumulative, and their effects worse, the more minority categories the affected person is in (e.g., a female, who is also from a minority ethnicity, who is also neurodivergent, and in a same-gender relationship, would be much worse off in a non-inclusive organisation than an ethnic majority, neurotypical, heterosexual female).

Some Examples of Subtle Dynamics May Include

- **Presentation:** Using words or phrases that contain overly masculine and/or culturally or ethnically excluding terms, such as "headhunting", "penetrating the market", or "subordinate".

- **Isolation:** Decisions made that exclude the input of the person they would affect most directly or who would be responsible for taking ownership of the outcome.

- **Slights:** Minimising the ideas, perspectives or preferences of a person in a way that leaves them feeling ignored, labelled, brushed off or disabled rather than enabled, heard and valued (e.g., telling someone they are "too rough", "not mature" or "too emotional" or requiring them to "go write a 5,000-word essay on how we can make this work" (which is not actually read or actioned).

- **Recognition:** Losing credit for ideas, not being thanked or acknowledged while others are, or experiencing a need to consistently validate one's credentials.

- **Stereotype threats:** The fear of emphasising negative stereotypes about an identity category to which one belongs. A brilliant social experiment covered by Joshua Aronson and his colleagues in their article "When White Men Can't do Math[44]" demonstrates the impact that communicating a message with stereotypes can have. In one example given by Aronson, Caucasian students were told they have "a maths test" and scored much higher compared to when they were told they have "a maths test to assess how Asians are better at maths than white students."

So, how do I know if my team members are being subjected to subtle dynamics and/or stereotype threats? They are not pleasant, nor are they always obvious, but here are some signs to look out for to help identify victims of subtle dynamics or stereotyping:

- Not speaking up in certain meetings.

- Being reluctant to take the lead or stepping down unexpectedly from leadership positions.

- Being harsh in evaluating their work and discounting their own performance while giving credit to others.

- Not respecting their own rest time/time off.

- Constantly being "connected", even when they don't need to be (during weekends, holidays, out of working hours, etc.)

Some of the above behaviours can be attributed to a lack of confidence or experience or even to hyperfocus or other issues. However, if this is the same person you interviewed and they have previous experience working in other jobs similar to this one, then the behaviours above could be signs of coping and masking mechanisms that even the most experienced people will show when subtle dynamics and stereotype threats trigger them.

Now, with more of a focus on autism specifically, here are a few other things that can demonstrate unconscious bias and allow it to be weaponised against autistic individuals.

Categorising individuals as part of an underrepresented group can result in unconscious bias, rendering essentialism useless in solving autism-related issues. When someone states that they don't understand an autistic individual's "way of speaking" or "type", it is critical to clarify which aspect of their identity they are referring to in order to bridge the gap. Humans are more similar than they are different, and it is crucial to remember this before creating an "us versus them" mentality.

Minimising an issue or writing off microaggressions as "part of the norm" can also cause harm to those who are affected. It's not acceptable to say that someone's discriminatory comment was "just a joke", or that it was a "normal" point of view to express, or that the person who has been victimised by it is "taking it too seriously". Dismissing the gravity of an autistic person's experiences can cause them to feel marginalised and may result in further harm; offering a safe space to share and listen is essential to avoid gaslighting. Similarly, if a neurodivergent

UNCONSCIOUS BIAS AND BUSTING IT

colleague struggles with a task, it's unproductive to say that the task is "normal" and to encourage them to get better at it. Instead, offer additional training or try to identify other areas of strength that better fit the autistic person's skills.

In conclusion, assigning change efforts solely to the underrepresented group is likely to be ineffective. It is critical to understand and address the underlying causes of the issue, rather than just the symptoms. Placing the responsibility of fixing a problem solely on the individual can exacerbate bias, and asking a neurodivergent person and/or other minorities to be more assertive or confident fails to recognise the societal and cultural pressures that may hinder their ability to do so. Moreover, there are often benefits to behaving less assertively, especially for those who may face backlash for being too assertive, such as being stigmatised as "different" or "less likeable". Instead of placing the burden solely on the individual, it's essential to address systemic issues and recognise the impact of societal norms.

We need to acknowledge and accept that while some managers are brilliant, that does not guarantee that they will also be aware of their own biases or biases affecting others in their team as those biases may be unconscious and can go undetected in many cases. Even the best managers can't be expected to be effective bias disrupters if they haven't acquired the training or experience with it yet. The first step towards combatting bias is learning to acknowledge it, so that it can be recognised and responded to effectively. We hope this bonus chapter has served as a strong first step in working to initiate that process!

Realising that Bias Exists in:
- Our society
- Our systems
- Our selves

Recognizing Bias
- Subtle dynamics
- Institutional barriers

Responding to Bias
- Through more inclusive presentation
- Confront & eliminate exclusive practices
- Active inclusion

Figure 5: Recognising and responding to bias

BONUS, BONUS CHAPTER

Tips for Parents with Kids on the Spectrum

In this second bonus chapter, we will explore some practical strategies for creating an inclusive and supportive environment for children on the spectrum. By understanding and accommodating their unique characteristics, we can promote their well-being, academic success and social integration, resulting in a more amiable journey for the parents. Let's delve into some important tips and insights tailored specifically for younger autistic individuals to better support the coming generation.

- **Identifying motivators:** Understanding what motivates an autistic child is crucial for their engagement, positive behaviour and positive reinforcement. While neurotypical children may find motivation in activities like sharing toys or having free playtime, autistic children often find motivation in their own unique interests and preferences. By identifying and utilising these meaningful motivators, such as their special interests or favourite foods, we can effectively encourage desired behaviours, gently redirect negative behaviours and foster a sense of accomplishment.

- **Sensory considerations:** Autistic children often experience sensory sensitivities that can significantly impact their comfort and engagement, both at home and inside the classroom. To create a more supportive environment for them, it is crucial to recognise their individual sensory preferences and aversions so those can be accommodated as needed. For example, for some autistic children, holding hands can be an overwhelming experience due to factors like warmth, wetness or dryness. Offering alternative options, such as holding onto a teacher's belt or a hand scarf instead, can provide a sense of security without triggering discomfort or over-whelm.

- **Individualised activities:** Just like neurotypical children, autistic children have diverse interests and preferences when it comes to activities and play; however, it is important for adults to recognise the role that their children's sensory sensitivities can have in determining those preferences. While some children may enjoy playing with sand or bean bags or textured toys, others may find these experiences overwhelming or distressing. It is essential to provide children on the spectrum with a range of activity options and to respect each child's unique comfort level and choices. By offering them individualised activities and respecting their ability to determine their own comfort level, we can foster inclusivity and promote engagement among autistic children.

- **Managing separation anxiety:** Transitioning to a new school or environment can be challenging for autistic children and may lead to heightened separation anxiety. Setting expectations may help to alleviate some of their distress; clear communication and visual supports can be highly beneficial in the transition process as well. Informing children that they will see their parents after school may help to prevent or reduce extreme separation anxiety, meltdowns and trauma; this can even be done while teaching them the concept of time by having them practice their understanding of the minute and hour hands on the clocks at school. Establishing consistent routines and visual schedules also provides children on the spectrum with a sense of predictability, aiding in a smoother transition.

- **Rewards and potential pitfalls:** Implementing a reward system can be effective in promoting positive behaviour in all children, neurotypical and neurodivergent alike. However, it is crucial to select rewards carefully, taking into account each child's unique needs and sensitivities. While some autistic children may respond positively to short periods of phone or tablet time, others may become overly fixated on screens and experience distress when access is restricted. Individualised reward systems ensure that positive reinforcement is tailored to each child's preferences, preventing potential pitfalls or setbacks before they can take place.

- **Post-school decompression:** Both school and work can be emotionally draining for autistic individuals, especially when the demands placed upon them by social and academic expectations are mixed with the sensory bombardments of all the noisy, colourful and unpredictable stimuli they experience during their classes. After a long day at school, children on the spectrum may require some time to decompress and recharge once they arrive back home. It is important to create a quiet and calm space where they can relax and engage in activities that help them unwind. Minimising demands and allowing them some downtime before engaging in further conversations or activities after school can help to prevent meltdowns or emotional outbursts.

- **The masking phenomenon:** Some autistic children may be highly skilled at masking their challenges in social and educational settings. However, as more demands are placed on them, their ability to maintain this façade may diminish. It is essential for educators and caregivers to be both vigilant and attentive to signs of increasing stress in autistic children as prolonged masking can lead to trauma and mental health issues in children as well as adults. Creating a supportive and understanding environment, where children can unmask and be their authentic selves without fear of judgement, is crucial for their well-being.

- **Individualised support:** Autistic children often require individualised attention and support due to the unique challenges they face in sensory, academic and social domains. Providing them with one-on-one assistance whenever possible can help address their specific needs and foster their overall development, without their having to worry about all the social and sensory issues that come hand in hand with a big classroom. This personalised approach to support will allow for tailored instruction and increased engagement for the child as well as a better understanding of each child's strengths and areas for improvement for educators and caregivers.

Conclusion

As with supporting adults in the workplace, supporting autistic children in educational settings requires an understanding and acceptance of their unique needs, challenges and characteristics. Just as autistic adults may struggle to navigate the social and sensory challenges of a workplace built for neurotypicals, autistic children are left to find their way through a school system that has been designed without their comfort or preferences in mind. However, by implementing strategies that accommodate sensory sensitivities, individualise activities, manage separation anxiety, identify meaningful motivators, select appropriate rewards, allow for post-school decompression and provide individualised support, we can create an inclusive and supportive environment that promotes their well-being and success.

Would you like us to train, consult or speak at your next event on the topics of diversity, inclusion or Neuroinclusion?

We deliver insightful, lived experience, professional, heart-felt presentations that enable and inspire audiences to take actionable and practical steps to neuroinclusion.

With a mix of lived experiences, technology, humour and proven strategies and processes to evolve and enable your organisation to be more inclusive, our sessions are sure to be the highlight of your inclusion and neuroinclusion goals and calendar.

To learn more or to book us for your next event, visit: www.b-insight.co.uk

References

[1] O'Nions, E., Petersen, I., Buckman, J. E. J., Charlton, R., Cooper, C., Corbett, A., Happé, F., Manthorpe, J., Richards, M., Sauders, R., Zanker, C., Mandy, W., & Stott, J. (2023). Autism in England: Assessing underdiagnosis in a population-based cohort study of prospectively collected primary care data. *The Lancet Regional Health – Europe*, 29, 100626.

[2] United Nations (2006). Convention on the rights of persons with disabilities. Retrieved from https://www.un.org/development/desa/disabilities/convention-on-the-rights-of-persons-with-disabilities.html

[3] Kelly, R., & Mutebi, N. (2023). Invisible disabilities in education and employment. UK Parliament. Retrieved from https://post.parliament.uk/research-briefings/post-pn-0689/

[4] Singer, J. (2016). *NeuroDiversity: The birth of an idea* (2nd ed.)

[5] Singer, J. (2019). Reflections on neurodiversity. https://neurodiversity2.blogspot.com/p/what.html

[6] Armstrong, T. (2011). *The power of neurodiversity: unleashing the advantages of your differently wired brain* (1st Da Capo Press paperback ed.). Cambridge, MA: Da Capo Lifelong.

[7] Botha, M., Hanlon, J., Williams, G. L. (2021). Does language matter? Identity-first versus person-first language use in autism research: A response to Vivante. *Journal of Autism and Developmental Disorders.* Advance.

[8] Tel Aviv University, news release, Jan. 29, 2023.

[9] Happé, F., & Frith, U. (1996). The neuropsychology of autism. *Brain.* OUP. 119 (4), 1377–1400.

[10] Pearson, A., & Rose, K. (2020). A conceptual analysis of autistic masking.

[11] National Autistic Society. (2021). Stimming. Retrieved from https://www.autism.org.uk/advice-and-guidance/topics/behaviour/stimming

[12] Happé, F., & Frith, U. (2006). The weak coherence account: detail-focused cognitive style in autism spectrum disorders. *Journal of Autism and Developmental Disorders,* 36(1), 5–25.

[13] Baron-Cohen, S., Ashwin, E., Ashwin, C., Tavassoli, T., & Chakrabarti, B. (2017). Talent in autism: hyper-systemizing, hyper-attention to detail and sensory hypersensitivity. *Philosophical Transactions of the Royal Society B: Biological Sciences*, 372(1713), 20160154.

[14] Klin, A., Saulnier, C. A., Sparrow, S. S., Cicchetti, D. V., Volkmar, F. R., & Lord, C. (2007). Social and

communication abilities and disabilities in higher functioning individuals with autism spectrum disorders: The Vineland and the ADOS. *Journal of Autism and Developmental Disorders,* 37(4), 748–759.

[15] Wing, L., & Gould, J. (1979). Severe impairments of social interaction and associated abnormalities in children: epidemiology and classification. *Journal of Autism and Developmental Disorders,* 9(1), 11–29.

[16] Ehlers, S., & Gillberg, C. (1993). The epidemiology of Asperger syndrome: a total population study. *Journal of Child Psychology and Psychiatry,* 34(8), 1327–1350.

[17] Leekam, S. R., Nieto, C., Libby, S. J., Wing, L., & Gould, J. (2007). Describing the sensory abnormalities of children and adults with autism. *Journal of Autism and Developmental Disorders,* 37(5), 894–910. https://doi.org/10.1007/s10803-006-0218-7).

[18] Hill, E. L. (2004). Executive dysfunction in autism. *Trends in Cognitive Sciences,* 8(1), 26–32. https://doi.org/10.1016/j.tics.2003.11.003

[19] Happé, F., & Frith, U. (2006). The weak coherence account: Detail-focused cognitive style in autism spectrum disorders. *Journal of Autism and Developmental Disorders,* 36(1), 5–25.

[20] Klin, A., Jones, W., Schultz, R., Volkmar, F., & Cohen, D. (2002). Visual fixation patterns during viewing of naturalistic social situations as predictors of social competence in individuals with autism. *Archives of General Psychiatry,* 59(9), 809–816.

[21] Klin, A., Jones, W., Schultz, R., Volkmar, F., & Cohen, D. (2002). Visual fixation patterns during viewing of naturalistic social situations as predictors of social competence in individuals with autism. *Archives of General Psychiatry*, 59(9), 809–816.

[22] Chevallier, C., Kohls, G., Troiani, V., Brodkin, E. S., & Schultz, R. T. (2012). The social motivation theory of autism. *Trends in Cognitive Sciences*, 16(4), 231–239.

[23] Hurlbutt, K., & Chalmers, L. (2004). Adults with autism speak out: perceptions of their life experiences. *Focus on Autism and Other Developmental Disabilities*, 19(2), 113–118.

[24] Hallett, V., Lecavalier, L., Sukhodolsky, D. G., Cipriano, N., Aman, M. G., McCracken, J. T., & Vitiello, B. (2013). Exploring the manifestations of anxiety in children with autism spectrum disorders. *Journal of Autism and Developmental Disorders*, 43(10), 2341–2352.

[25] City & Guilds (2023). Increasing neurodiversity in the workplace: City & Guilds neurodiversity index report.

[26] Hull, L., Mandy, W., & Lai, M. C. (2019). Evidence for overlap between autism and ADHD: A systematic review and meta-analysis. *Journal of Autism and Developmental Disorders*, 49(12), 4645–4661.

[27] Fox, K. (2005). *Watching the English*, London: Hodder & Stoughton.

[28] Milton, D. (2012). On the ontological status of autism: The 'double empathy problem'. *Disability and Society*, 27(3), 883–887.

[29] The Institution of Engineering and Technology (2021) "Engineering and tech giants join forces to STEM £1.5bn annual skills gap".

[30] Baron-Cohen, S., Wheelwright, S., Burtenshaw, A., & Hobson, E. V. (2001). The autism-spectrum quotient: Evidence from Asperger syndrome/high-functioning autism, males and females, scientists and mathematicians. *Journal of Autism and Developmental Disorders*, 31(1), 5–17.

[31] Ruzich, E., Allison, C., Smith, P., Watson, P., Auyeung, B., Ring, H., & Baron-Cohen, S. (2015). Sex and STEM occupation predict autism-spectrum quotient (AQ) scores in half a million people. *PloS ONE*, 10(10), e0141229.

[32] Marsack-Topolewski, C. N., Franz, L., Aggarwal, R., & Weiss, J. A. (2019). Understanding STEM career choices of autistic adults: A survey study. *Autism Research*, 12(9), 1388–1399.

[33] Sala, R., Amet, L., Blagojevic-Stokic, N, Shattock, P., & Whiteley, P. (2020). Bridging the gap between physical health and autism spectrum disorder. *Neuropsychiatric Disease and Treatment*, 30,16, 1605–1618.

[34] City & Guilds (2023). Increasing neurodiversity in the workplace: City & Guilds neurodiversity index report.

[35] O'Hora, D., McKernan, J., & McNicholas, F. (2020). Autism and the experience of trauma. *European Psychiatry*, 63(1), e6. doi:10.1192/j.eurpsy.2020.4

[36] Soke, M. (2018). Microaggressions and Autism: An Unexamined Social Concern.

[37] Treffert, D. A. (2009). The savant syndrome: An extraordinary condition. A synopsis past, present, and future. *Philosophical Transactions of the Royal Society Series B, Biological Sciences*, 364(1522), 1351–1357.

[38] Sriganthan, A. (2023). Two thirds of UK neurodivergent employees fear discrimination at work, research finds. People Management.

[39] Cholteeva, Y. (2023). Three quarters of HR professionals have not had specific neurodiversity training in the last 12 months, study finds. People Management.

[40] See the podcasts and posts of Professor Nancy Doyle (Genius Within). Available at https://geniuswithin.org/

[41] Nicholas, L., Brook, L., & Fox, J. (2020). Autism and the workplace: A review of the research literature. *Autism*, 24(2), 203–217. doi:10.1177/1362361319863204

[42] McKinsey & Company. (2015). Why diversity matters. Available at https://www.mckinsey.com/capabilities/people-and-organizational-performance/our-insights/why-diversity-matters

[43] Williams, J. C., Korn, R. M., Mihaylo, S. (2020). Beyond implicit bias: Litigating race and gender employment discrimination using data from the workplace experiences survey, *Hastings Law Journal*, 72,1, 337–464.

[44] Aronson, J., Lustina, M. J., Good, C., Keough, K., Steele, C. M., & Brown, J. (1999). When white men can't do math: Necessary and sufficient factors in stereotype

threats. *Journal of Experimental Social Psychology*, 35, 29–46.